Teaching Children to Listen

Resources available for download

All material in the Appendices and coloured versions of the illustrations are available online at www.continuumbooks.com/resources/9781441174765.

Please visit the link and register with us to receive your password and access to thses downloadable resources.

If you experience any problems accessing the resources, please contact Continuum at info@continuumbooks.com

Also available from Continuum:

Foundations of Literacy – Ros Bayley and Sue Palmer
Lend Us Your Ears – Rosemary Sage
Language and Communication Difficulties – Dimitri Hartas
100 Ideas for Teaching Communication, Language and Literacy – Susan Elkin
Toon Cards: A Multi Purpose Resource for Developing Communication Skills – Chris Terrell

Teaching Children to Listen

A practical approach to
developing children's listening skills

Liz Spooner and Jacqui Woodcock

continuum

Continuum International Publishing Group

The Tower Building	80 Maiden Lane, Suite 704
11 York Road	New York
London	NY 10038
SE1 7NX	

www.continuumbooks.com

British Library Cataloguing-in-Publication Data
A catalogue record for this book is available from the British Library.

ISBN: 9781441174765 (paperback)

Library of Congress Cataloging-in-Publication Data
To come

Typeset by Free Range Book Design & Production Limited
Printed and bound in Great Britain by the MPG Books Group

ABOUT THE AUTHORS

Liz Spooner is a Speech and Language Therapist specialising in specific language impairment. She has 19 years of experience of working in education.

Jacqui Woodcock is a Speech and Language Therapist and the leader of a paediatric Speech and Language Therapy team. She has worked in nurseries and schools in the area for over 16 years.

Liz and Jacqui both have many years of experience in running groups with children and in providing training workshops for their colleagues in education. They have both worked for the National Health Service for over 20 years and are currently employed by Worcestershire Primary Care Trust.

jacquelinewoodcock@nhs.net
l.spooner@nhs.net

ACKNOWLEDGEMENTS

With our thanks to the children of Lickey Hills Primary School, Rednal, Birmingham and St Stephen's C of E First School, Redditch for their help with the photos in this book.

CONTENTS

1   Why work on listening?

From our work in schools we are seeing increasing numbers of children who find it challenging to keep listening, stay focused on a task and follow even simple instructions in the classroom. This poor listening affects their learning in all curriculum areas – and their resultant distractible behaviour can also make it more difficult for the rest of the class to keep listening.

Is there evidence that children's listening really has deteriorated?

It is difficult to find evidence to back up the perception that children's listening skills have declined rapidly in recent years for the simple reason that historically, children's listening skills have not been measured or recorded, and so we have no established norms with which today's children can be compared. What there is no shortage of, however, is anecdotal evidence. A review of the recent research into listening reflects the concerns that are being voiced by teachers in schools throughout the country:

- In 2001 the National Literacy Trust and the National Association of Head Teachers carried out a survey which asked head teachers for their views on children's speaking and listening skills. The results showed that 74% of people responding felt that children's speaking and listening skills had declined in the past five years.

- Two years later in 2003, the Basic Skills Agency surveyed 716 head teachers about the children starting their reception classes. The results showed that 60% felt that fewer than half of the 5-year-olds had the basic speaking and listening skills necessary when starting school.

- As a result of growing concerns over children's listening skills, the *Times Educational Supplement* carried out an analysis of 350 Ofsted inspection reports. This analysis showed that inspectors were concerned about the speaking and listening skills of around half of the 4 and 5-year-olds starting school in September 2003.

The trends described in these surveys were anticipated in pioneering research in the 1980s carried out by Dr Sally Ward, principal speech and language therapist working for Central Manchester Healthcare Trust. Her research with babies under one year in 1984 showed that one in five had attention and listening difficulties. However, by 1990 the incidence of listening difficulties had doubled. This is a frightening rate of decline and there appears to be plenty of evidence that listening skills have continued to deteriorate.

Why do so many children find it so hard to listen now?

It is less clear what the reasons for the decline in listening skills might be. It is not likely that one factor alone is responsible for the deterioration in children's listening and it is much more likely that this is the result of a complex interaction of cultural changes. Factors which might be relevant are:

- **The constant availability of screen-based entertainment**
  The perceived deterioration in listening skills has taken place at the same time that we have witnessed a massive increase in the time children spend facing a screen, whether it be a TV or a computer. According to the British Market Research Bureaux, children aged 11–15 now spend 55% of their waking hours either watching TV or using a computer. This is an astonishing 53 hours a week and represents a 40% increase over the previous decade (BMRB 2004). By the time the average child reaches their sixth birthday they will already have spent a whole year of their life watching television.
    An influential 2004 retrospective study of over 1200 children in the USA which was carried out by Christakis et al. looked at the relationship between early television exposure and subsequent attentional problems in children. This study found significant listening difficulties in 10% of 7-year-olds included in the study. It also found that for every extra hour of television watched as a pre-schooler, the children had a 10% additional risk of developing attention difficulties.

- **Changes in the way children play and learn to interact**
  Alongside the rise in screen-based entertainment has come a decline in more traditional play activities. Children playing together are now likely to watch a video or play a computer game rather than to engage in pretend play, and this reduces both the need for interactive skills and the opportunity to practise them.

- **Increased noise levels in the home during the crucial time when children are learning to talk**
  There is a significant amount of research which shows that even moderate background noise can distract very young children. A 2005 USA study of 7-month-olds, by Hollich et al. found that 'background noise in the average household – such as other children playing or watching television – can pose the same problem for children that an older adult with hearing loss encounters at a cocktail party'. This study was the first to show that even low levels of background noise can affect a child's ability to listen. A more recent study (2008) by Evans, Schmidt et al. found that background television significantly affected children's attention to play, even when they appeared not to be watching it. A further study by Kirkorian et al. found that 'both the quantity and quality of parent-child interaction decreased in the presence of background television'. This would not be a big issue if the television was rarely on but Rideout et al. (2005) found that in 51% of households the television was on 'most of the time' and in 63% of homes the television was 'usually' on during mealtimes. In summary, most children are now learning to communicate against a continual level of background noise which has been shown both to affect both their own attention and how well their parents interact with them.

- **A reduction in the time that families spend talking and listening to each other**
  The past generation has been one of revolutionary cultural change with 55% of women with children under five now working outside the home, compared with 25% in 1975. This means that more young children are spending time in childcare where opportunities for one-to-one interactions may be more limited. Additionally, the pace of modern life means that parents have less time to interact with their family. A 2006 I CAN survey found that parents spent more time both watching television and doing housework than they did communicating with their children.
    The reasons behind the perceived decline in children's listening are likely to be complex and far-reaching but what is clear is that by 2006 concerns were at such a level that I CAN (the charity working to improve the speech, language and communication of children) carried out detailed research looking at speaking and listening skills in both children and adults. As a result I CAN produced the document *The Cost to the Nation of Children's Poor Communication*. It stated that upwards of 50% of children entering school were identified as having some kind of communication difficulty.
    During our own work in mainstream first schools in Bromsgrove and Redditch in 2007–2009, we asked teachers to rate the listening skills of the children in their class to see if national concerns were reflected locally. Figure 1.1 summarises the listening skills of 1101 children and shows that teachers rated only around a third of the children in their classes as having adequate listening skills to access the curriculum.

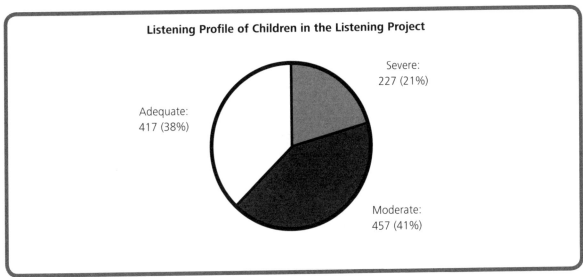

Listening Profile of Children in the Listening Project

Severe:
227 (21%)

Adequate:
417 (38%)

Moderate:
457 (41%)

Figure 1.1. Teachers' rating of the listening skills 1101 children in Worcestershire first schools 2007–2009

Analysis of listening patterns in individual classes also revealed two interesting trends:

o Teachers working with classes from reception to Year 4 (children aged 4 to 9 years) were asked to rate their classes. The proportion of adequate listeners did not change significantly as children moved through school. This suggests that exposure to the school environment alone is not effective in helping children to learn how to listen.
o Despite schools working with a wide range of children (ranging from children from affluent backgrounds to those from homes in areas of economic deprivation) the proportion of adequate to inadequate listeners in classes did not vary significantly. This suggests that listening difficulties are affecting children from a range of socio-economic backgrounds.

Why is good listening important?

In 2006 we were approached by a group of head teachers in Worcestershire who had been allocated money from the Extended Schools initiative and wanted to raise the levels of speaking and listening amongst their children. We were very keen to offer a programme that would be of benefit to all children rather than just the few who might be referred to speech and language therapy. We decided that we could make the most impact by offering a whole-school approach to improving listening skills. This is because listening underpins all language development. Development of early listening skills in the first few months of life is necessary for children successfully to understand and use language.

Figure 1.2 illustrates how listening is the foundation block for all language and communication development:

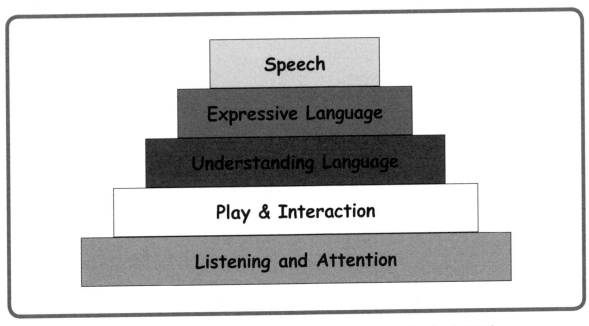

Figure 1.2. Building Blocks of Language (A. Williams & J. Woodcock 2008)

The figure shows that learning to listen is vital in developing the ability to play and interact with others successfully. It underpins the development of understanding language and talking. Listening skills are necessary to acquire all the speech sounds we need to use when talking. Later, when starting school, all these foundation blocks need to be in place in order for children successfully to develop literacy skills.

Children are often referred to speech and language therapy because of concerns over language or literacy. After assessment, it often becomes apparent that the real issue that needs to be addressed is their listening, which is a much earlier stage in language development. Poor listening affects children's ability to learn across the whole curriculum. We have all worked with children attempting a task at an appropriate level for their academic ability but not succeeding. However, the reason they are unable to succeed is because of their poor listening skills.

In addition, poor listeners are more likely to be restless and their behaviour can make it more difficult for the rest of the class. They also find it more difficult to play and interact with others. Children who have not learned to stay quiet when other people are talking and listen to what they are saying find it more difficult to form successful social relationships. Home Office findings in 2004 indicated that around 35% of offenders in Britain had speaking and listening skills below those expected of an 11-year-old (Davis et al. 2004).

Recognition by policy makers

In Britain, experts in child development and education are now recognising the crucial role that listening has to play. In 2006, the Review of the Teaching of Early Reading carried out for the Department for Education and Skills by Jim Rose recommended that 'far more attention needs to be given, right from the start, to promoting speaking and listening skills to make sure that children build a good stock of words, learn to listen attentively and speak clearly and confidently'. The government recognised growing concern over children's listening and language levels in its *Framework for Teaching Literacy* (2006) which makes explicit the centrality of speaking and listening, not only as a communicative skill in its own right, but also as the bedrock of literacy development. The 2006 I CAN paper *The Cost to the Nation of Children's Poor Communication* concludes 'many children with either transient or persistent communication difficulties can go on to learn, socialise and communicate confidently if they are supported in the right way and at the right time'.

In 2008, *The Bercow Report: A Review of Services for Children and Young People with Speech, Language and Communication Needs* looked at services for children with identified difficulties but also stated that there was a need for 'universal services to support the speech, language and communication development of all children'. In its response to the Bercow review, the National Literacy Trust stated that 'the NLT firmly believes that literacy is composed of speaking, listening, reading and writing, with speaking and listening skills fundamental to any success in reading and writing'.

Developing an effective approach

In our work with children we have felt, in many cases, that the issue was not that they were unable to listen, but rather that they did not understand what good listening meant. With this in mind, we devised an approach to teach listening skills explicitly using activities that could be carried out with whole classes in school. This approach aimed to:

- teach children what good listening is
- show children why listening is important
- motivate children to do good listening independently.

The approach was piloted in seven schools in the local area and involved therapists working directly with whole classes, teaching listening skills for one lesson each week over a period of six weeks.

As this was a new way of working, it was important to evaluate whether the approach was effective in changing children's listening in the classroom. Teachers rated the listening of children in their classes before and after the intervention. (See chapter 3 for more information on evaluating children's listening skills.) To maximise objectivity, when teachers rated the second time, they did not have access to their original ratings. The Listening Rating Scale used by the teachers can be found in appendix 2. Figure 1.3 shows the children's listening scores before and after intervention.

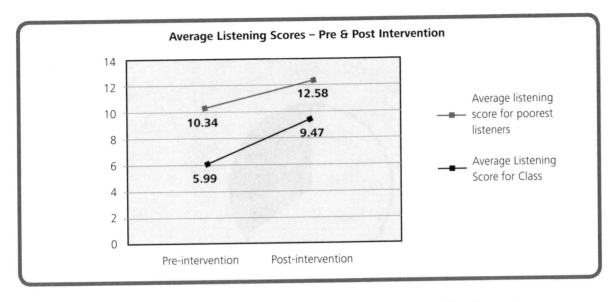

Figure 1.3. Average listening scores before and after whole-class listening work

The average listening score for all children increased by over 2 points (21.7%) but the average improvement in listening scores for those children rated as 'severe' was over 3 points (58.1%).

We used the teachers' ratings to classify children in the following way:

- A score of below 8 indicates a **severe listening difficulty**.
- A score between 8 and 11 indicates a **moderate listening difficulty**.
- A score between 12 and 16 indicates **adequate listening skills**.

Figures 1.4 and 1.5 show the impact that intervention has on the listening profile of whole-class populations.

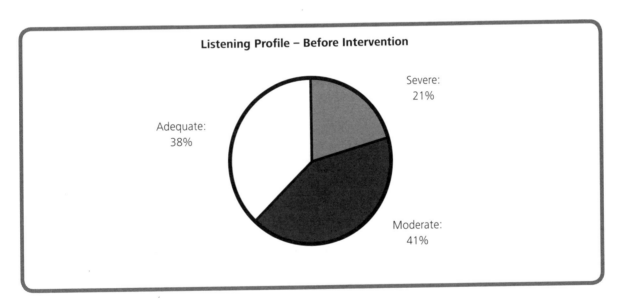

Figure 1.4. Listening Profile of classes before whole-class listening work – sample size 1101 children

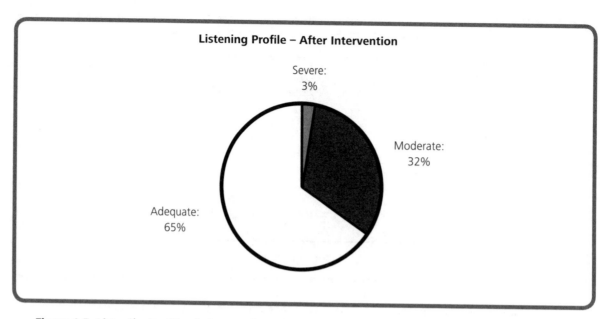

Figure 1.5. Listening Profile of classes after whole-class listening work – sample size 1101 children

Where possible, we returned to schools a term later to determine whether the improvements in listening had been sustained. Re-ratings by teachers showed that not only had children maintained the progress in listening, but in many cases their listening had continued to improve.

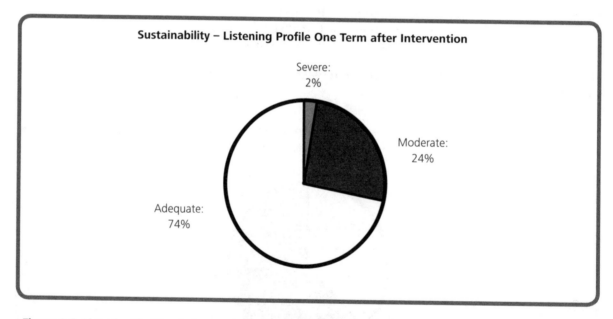

Figure 1.6. Listening Profile of classes one term after whole-class listening work – sample size 673 children

The results exceeded our expectations and showed that children can make real progress in learning to listen with a limited amount of targeted input. The activities described in the following chapters have enabled children to:

- develop an understanding of what good listening means
- experience and learn from situations where they have to carry out each component of good listening to be successful
- be motivated to do good listening throughout the school day

Despite the initial concerns of the teachers we worked with, once children understood what we were asking them to do when listening, and had appropriate expectations placed on them, they were able to change their own behaviour to listen effectively.

2   What is good listening?

From our experience of working with children, it has become apparent that there are four different behaviours that children need to learn in order to be a good listener:

- **Look at the person who is talking.**
- **Sit still.**
- **Stay quiet so that everyone can listen.**
- **Listen to ALL of the words.**

Cue cards for all of these rules can be found in appendix 1.

Looking at the person who is talking

It is important to establish that the rule is 'Looking at the *person* who is talking' rather than 'Looking at the teacher'. Some children can learn that they need to look at the teacher but then do not generalise this skill to other people in other situations. We want children to be good listeners in all situations so they need to learn that they have to look at the speaker at all times and this could be other children, different members of staff, their lunchtime supervisors or members of their family. Many learning situations in school require children to work in groups, where they need to listen and respond to other children in order to carry out a task successfully. Another reason to encourage children to look is that it helps them gain more information. Professionals who work with children tend to be very skilled at using non-verbal communication, facial expression and gesture to get their message across. However, all this extra effort is wasted on children who have not learned the value of eye contact.

What about the children who don't appear to be listening because they don't look?

We have all worked with children like this, who, when they are questioned, show that they have listened to all of the words even though they weren't looking. We would still challenge this behaviour as looking is the way we show we are interested in what the speaker is saying and is therefore an important social skill to establish.

Sitting still

What we are aiming for with the children that we work with is appropriate balanced sitting with no fidgeting. However, in our experience, children often have very little insight into how well (or badly!) they are sitting. Appropriate sitting reduces distractions for children and enables them to focus more easily on what the speaker is saying. Many children distract not only themselves but others when they fidget, so reducing this kind of behaviour will improve the listening of the whole class.

Staying quiet

If this rule can be established with a group of children, it will have a huge impact on the listening environment for everyone. This is because children who shout out always disrupt other people's listening as well as their own. Children find it hard to conform to this rule in a number of ways. Some children can shout out comments that are irrelevant to the lesson, e.g. 'It's my birthday tomorrow!' Other children may hum or tap, which is less obviously intrusive but may still distract other children. The most difficult group of children to deal with are those who shout out answers or comments that are relevant to the topic. These children are often bright and haven't been identified as having difficulties with listening. Although it is positive that they are engaged by the topic, when they shout out they are disrupting the processing of other children who take longer to find the answer. Learning to wait for your turn before speaking is a social skill children need both in formal learning situations and in conversations.

Listening to ALL of the words

This is a rule that is important to establish for a number of reasons. The following things can go wrong:

- Children may not follow instructions given to the whole class and will only listen if they are called by name.
- Children may listen to the first part of an instruction, think they know what to do, and then stop listening.
- With a familiar activity, children may not listen at all as they have already experienced the task and think they know what to do.
- Some instructions may contain a 'trigger phrase' such as 'Line up at the door' or 'It's nearly dinnertime.' When children hear this, they don't pay attention to anything else.

When teaching this rule, we try to put children in situations where they have to listen to <u>all</u> of the words in order to carry out the task successfully.

Normal development of listening

Many of the listening skills children can struggle with when they get to school, should have developed in the first few months of life (Murkoff et al. 2004):

- **At birth:** Babies can recognise their mother's voice because they have heard it while they were in the womb.
- **At 1 month:** Babies should be able to focus on a face and make eye contact. However many children come to school still not realising that eye contact is a useful skill which will help them to gain more information from the speaker.
- **At 4 months:** Babies should be able to take part in a 'cooing conversation'. This means that they are beginning to understand the idea of turn taking – they make a noise, the other person makes a noise, they make a noise again. This is a really early skill which develops well before spoken language and yet many children start school without understanding that, in order to listen, they need to stay quiet when the other person is talking.
- **At 7 months:** Babies should turn in the direction of a voice in preference to other noises. This is a key skill for listening. As adults we are able to filter out irrelevant noise and focus on the most important sound – usually a voice. Some children have great difficulty developing this ability and consequently are continually distracted by intrusive noises that the adult may not even be aware of.
- **At 10 months:** By now, babies should be really skilled at turn taking with an adult using gestures and babble.
- **At 12 months:** Babies should be able to turn in response to their name. However, many children much older than this know their name but do not respond to it unless it is said several times, often with increasing volume!

So, many of the skills needed for good listening should have developed well before the child can even talk. If a child starts school and these abilities are not in place then saying 'Listen to me' is just not going to be enough. The child does not understand what good listening is and does not have the skills necessary to do it. Our experience is that, by this stage, these skills need to be explicitly taught if they are ever going to develop.

3 Identifying what is going wrong

We can usually recognise when children are not doing good listening but it can be more difficult to identify exactly what they are doing wrong. The Listening Skills Rating Scale is quick to use and allows you to rate children on each of the four rules of good listening.

	Score	1	2	3	4
Sitting still		Not able to stay on chair/floor Constant fidgeting	Inappropriate sitting posture/ lots of fidgeting	Stays on chair/ floor but some fidgeting	Appropriate balanced sitting
Looking at the person who is talking		Does not initiate eye contact spontaneously	Some eye contact but not sustained	Initiates eye contact but needs recall	Appropriate eye contact when listening
Staying quiet		Consistently interrupts/talks during instructions	Occasionally quiet but cannot maintain this	Some talking but can be recalled to stay quiet and listen	Quiet when listening in class
Listening to all of the words		Does not follow instructions/relies on routine/copies others Does not recognise when has not understood	Carries out part of an instruction – needs repeated reminders	Follows simple instructions but needs repetition of complex information	Able to listen to complex/ unfamiliar information
			Recognises when has not listened accurately and seeks help		

Figure 3.1. Listening Rating Scale. This is available for you to photocopy and use in appendix 2

By using the Rating Scale you can obtain an individual score for each of the four components of listening, and a total score. In our work with children we have classified scores in the following way.

A score of below 8:	Severe Listening Difficulties
A score of between 8 and 11:	Moderate Listening Difficulties
A score of 12 and above:	Adequate Listening Skills

The Rating Scale enables children's listening to be objectively measured and allows you to target direct work on the areas of listening where it is most needed. Some children have difficulties in all four areas of listening. Others may show more specific difficulties. During our work in schools we often see two types of poor listeners:

The active poor listener

These children are easy to spot. They score particularly poorly on 'Staying quiet' and 'Sitting still' but can show reasonable skills at 'Looking' and 'Listening to all of the words'. Their fidgeting behaviour means they can distract themselves and other children around them. They find it difficult to stay quiet but may be listening to what the teacher says and will shout out information relevant to the lesson topic. The problem is that when they shout out, they disrupt the processing of other children trying to listen. This behaviour also needs to be addressed because learning to wait for your turn before speaking is an important social skill that all children need to acquire.

The passive poor listener

These children are less noticeable in the classroom. They are usually quiet and can sit still during whole-class explanations or instructions. 'Looking' may be an area of difficulty but one that is difficult to spot when working with a large group of children. These children score particularly poorly on 'Listening to all of the words'. This often only becomes apparent when children have to carry out tasks following a whole-class instruction and, because they have not listened, they do not know what to do.

There is a Class Listening Profile to photocopy and use in appendix 3.

Setting SMART targets

The Rating Scale provides a tool to measure progress following direct input. It enables you to set specific targets in a number of ways.

1 Focusing on a specific area of difficulty

Setting targets for a specific rule that a child finds challenging helps to develop their insight into the behaviour they need to change. With children who have difficulties in all areas, choosing one rule to focus on increases their chance of achieving change quickly. Other rules can then become the focus.

Examples of specific rule targets are:

- Toby to achieve a rating of 3 for looking at the person who is talking during 'Show and Tell'
- Nathan to stay sitting still for 5 minutes during whole-class Literacy
- Kasey to keep quiet when other children are chosen to answer a question during maths
- Amy to listen to all the words in a question first, and then answer, when sharing her reading book.

2 Addressing listening in different contexts

Different learning environments in school create different challenges for children's listening. It is usually easiest for children to keep listening when working one-to-one. Small-group work is more difficult and listening during whole-class activities creates the biggest challenge. It can be helpful to set targets in less challenging environments and allow the child to experience some success before moving on to setting targets for listening in class. It may be too much to expect children to carry out their targets for a whole lesson. In this case, setting a target for a small amount of time such as 5 minutes will allow a child to achieve some success. You can then extend the amount of time that you are expecting them to carry out the behaviour.

- Ryan to stay quiet and sit still for 10 minutes while other children are reading in his shared reading group.
- Chris to achieve a rating of 3 for 'Listening to all of the words' when another child talks during paired maths work.
- Tom to look at the teacher when they call his name during register time.

Children on the autistic spectrum often learn skills in a very rigid and specific way. They can sometimes show good listening within their classroom or with a particular teacher. When working in a different part of the school, or with a different member of staff, it can be helpful to set explicit targets about listening to help them transfer their skills.

- Hannah to do good looking when we go into the hall for PE
- Max to stay quiet when we work in our phonics group with Mrs Jones.

3 Identifying particular challenges, and setting targets to overcome them

Children's listening can sometimes be affected by factors that adults can recognise but that the children themselves are unaware of. When this happens, it is helpful to set targets that address these factors.

- George to keep looking at the teacher when he is sitting next to the computer in class for 5 minutes
- Katie to keep listening to all of the words even when children are playing a game on the next table
- Andrew to stay sitting still when we use the number fans during maths.

4 Overcoming the problems of group mix

Teaching staff are always able to identify children who are not a good combination when they sit together. Unfortunately, when given the choice these children always want to be together. There are two ways of dealing with this. Firstly, you can separate them, but this means that you are managing the children's behaviour for them. Alternatively, you can be explicit about what happens when they sit together. E.g. 'When you sit together you talk and don't do good listening.' Unless we give children this feedback they are often unaware of why they have been separated. Then you can set them a specific listening target such as ' I'm going to see if you and Jack can stay quiet and keep looking at the white board even though you are sitting together.' Then at the end of the lesson you can negotiate with the children on how well they did. If they weren't able to achieve their target, explain this and sit them separately again.

Using the Rating Scale with children

In our experience, it is helpful to be explicit with children about the targets you are setting for them. Children often have little insight into their own listening behaviour, so you may need to describe and model what they are doing now, and the target behaviour you are aiming for, in order to help them to change.

With older children, it can be helpful to share the Rating Scale with them so that they can see what they need to change and what they are aiming for. Once a target has been agreed with a child, you will need to remind them of what they are expected to do at the beginning of each relevant lesson. E.g. 'Remember your target in this lesson is to stay quiet. What do you have to do if you have got something to say? Put up your hand and wait for the teacher to choose you.'

Using the Rating Scale with parents

In order for children to make good progress in listening, it is really helpful to get the support of their parents. Using the Rating Scale when sharing concerns with parents can help to give them some insight into their child's listening behaviour at school. When appropriate, specific targets can also be reinforced at home. For example:

- Parents can encourage the child to make eye contact when listening to instructions.
- Parents can remind children that staying quiet when someone else is talking will help them to listen.

Information on listening which can be shared with parents can be found in appendix 4.

4   How to use the activities

Who can you use the activities with?

The activities have primarily been used with children from about 3 to 11 years but using the 'make it harder' modifications will make the activities suitable for children older than this. Activities which are particularly suitable for Early Years are marked with this symbol:

We have also used these activities very successfully with children with learning difficulties and other special needs.

Who should lead the activities?

The activities are designed to be used by teachers, teaching assistants and therapists. However, it is important to remember, that although the activities appear simple, the children you use them with are not! Running these activities, particularly with larger groups, requires a high level of skill in managing behaviour. We have found that more experienced practitioners are more effective and confident when running the groups and so tend to get better results. If you are a less experienced practitioner, then it may be a good idea to start with a small group so you can become familiar with the activities without having to worry about crowd control.

We would also recommend that, whenever possible, groups are run with two adults. This may seem an expensive use of resources but it is justifiable in terms of the added effectiveness. Two adults working together enables:

- an adult to model the activities first
- one adult to monitor and deal with any behaviour issues, freeing the other adult to concentrate on leading the activity
- an adult to support by drawing the leader's attention to children who are trying hard, e.g. 'Mrs Smith you are going to be so proud of Sam. He is doing a really good job of looking at you and it's helping him to do really good listening.' They can also draw the leader's attention to children who are not showing good listening, e.g. 'Mr Brown, I'm worried that you won't be able to choose Kyle for this game because he keeps shouting out.'

Ideally, one of the adults leading the group should be someone who works with the children at other times. This may be their class teacher or teaching assistant. This really encourages the children to carry over their good listening to other situations and ensures that children know that the expectations of their listening in class will be high.

How many children should I have in my group?

All of the activities described in the following chapters have been used with whole classes of children. There are some benefits to this. Firstly, with a large group of children, it is impossible for everyone to have a turn and therefore the children must show good listening behaviour in order to get a turn. This is a very powerful lever and significantly increases motivation to conform. Secondly, if the whole class learns rules together, it ensures a common set of rules and expectations that is difficult to achieve if a small group is taken out of the class to work on listening.

In some situations, it may be useful to organise smaller groups. For example, this could be used to give extra practise to the children with the more severe listening difficulties or if you want to combine a group of pupils across year groups. We have often run mixed-age groups and found this to be an effective way of working, providing the age range is limited to two or three years.

If you are intending to run a smaller listening group, we would recommend that you select a minimum of six children to take part. If the group is too small the children will get a high level of adult attention and will not have to wait for a turn. Consequently, a small group does not usually put sufficient pressure on children's listening for difficulties to be apparent and for new skills to be learnt and generalised.

What should I do if children do not comply?

You will encounter two types of non-compliance:

Dealing with poor listeners

It is inevitable when running a group to improve listening that you will have children in your group who can't listen! These children often want to please you but are just not aware that they are fidgeting or shouting out. The best way to deal with this group of children is to be very explicit about what they are doing and what the target behaviour is. E.g. 'Tom, I really want to choose you for this game but I can't because you are shouting out at me. I'm going to really watch you next time to see if you can stay quiet.' Then watch for the child to show the target behaviour and praise them straight away. E.g. 'Tom, I'm so proud of you! I can choose you now – you stayed really quiet!' This is a very positive and effective way of helping these children to change their behaviour.

Dealing with deliberate disruption

The second group of children is much less common but more challenging to deal with. These are the children who are deliberately disruptive or who try to sabotage the games. Deliberate disruption has been a rare occurrence for us in running listening groups because the activities are all game based and children's motivation is usually very high. However, it is impossible to run the games successfully with a child being disruptive so this kind of behaviour must be dealt with before the game continues. There are two approaches to try:

- If you know the group well, you may be able to anticipate difficult behaviour before it occurs. In this case you can set the children a challenge 'Charlotte, I want to choose you for this game but I am worried that you might be a bit silly and try to make the children laugh. Can I trust you to be really sensible and do your best sitting?' or 'Boys, I need to hide this toy but I'm worried that if I put it behind you that you will turn around and look at it and that will spoil the game. Can I trust you to keep looking forward?' Obviously, it is then really important to praise them when they meet your challenge. In our experience, the vast majority of children want to please adults and when given a specific target they will rise to the challenge.

- You will not be able to forward plan for all deliberate disruption and if you are faced with a child who is behaving inappropriately then we would advise you to challenge this immediately. E.g. 'Connor, I'm sad because you spoiled the game then. We can't play this game if you are going to point. I need you to keep your hands still. Can you do that?' Then continue with the game. If they persist with the inappropriate behaviour then you will need to remove them from the game until they are ready to comply. It is important to be firm and consistent with disruptive behaviour if the activity is to be effective for the rest of the children in the group.

How do I make sure the game works?

There is no way to guarantee that a game will always be successful but our tips for success are:

- **Be a top model:** Always model the activity with an adult first so that the children know what the target behaviour is. This technique of showing as well as telling is good practice for all children, not just those with listening and language problems, and will steer the game successfully around numerous pitfalls.
- **Establish the ground rules:** However easy the games seem, take the time to read the 'Ground Rules' and 'Inside Information' before you start. We have played these games thousands of times and these sections should help you to learn from our mistakes and generally to get the most out of the games. Always take the time to establish the ground rules with the children before you start. E.g. 'Right – there are three things that we have to remember when we play this game …' Then make sure you enforce the rules. For example, if one of the ground rules is that everyone has to look at the person with the blindfold, then go around the circle checking that everyone is doing that before you take the blindfold off.
- **Learn to adapt:** Pitching the game at the right level can make the difference between success and failure. Use the 'Make it harder – Make it easier' suggestions to start the activity at the right level. If in doubt, start at the easier level and work up. If an activity seems to be too challenging then do not be afraid to swap to an easier version mid-game. It is better to do this than to keep going with an activity that is not working.

How can I help the children to generalise these listening skills to other situations?

Everyone who has ever taught children knows that teaching children a new skill is the easy part – getting them to use that skill in other situations, when you are not there, is the real challenge. Listening is no different. Demonstrating good listening skills in a group is no use at all if all the new skills disappear as soon as they are back in a usual classroom environment. Later chapters in this book will deal in more depth with strategies for the classroom but there are certain tactics that you can try when running the activities which will make generalisation more likely:

- Make it clear what children have to do in order to get a turn and stick to this both in the activities and class. If everyone gets a turn regardless of how they are behaving, then there is no incentive to listen. Make sure that children know that they need to sit still, be quiet and look at you in order to get a turn. If you can't give them a turn then explain why. E.g. 'Max, I'd love you choose you but I can't because you are not looking at me. What do you need to do to get a turn?'
- There is something very powerful in the children knowing that their teacher has seen them doing good listening and is expecting to see it again when it matters. You can exploit this with children in class by reminding them of what they achieved in the listening group. E.g. 'I know you can do good looking now. Can you show me that great looking while we do our science investigation?'
- Make links for the children to other situations where they could use the skills that they have practised. E.g. 'Sophie, you did a fantastic job of sitting still then! I'm going to watch to see if you can do that brilliant sitting when we have big book.'
- Set up teaching situations that emphasise the importance of good listening. For example:

    o Avoid choosing children to answer questions in a predictable order. Always going in sequence can encourage children to switch off once they have had a turn.
    o Explain that even when a child has had a turn they need to keep listening, as you might choose them again (and make sure you carry this out!).
    o Do a familiar activity in a different sequence but always be explicit about this before you start the activity.

How do I fit the activities into the timetable?

The activities can be used very flexibly. For example:

- one game each day in circle time
- one game each day to focus children at the start of Literacy
- small-group listening work as part of Special Needs provision
- whole-class listening group as part of relevant lessons such as PHSE.

A combination of all of the above could be used. If possible, we would recommend starting any new approach to listening with a specific listening group. This gives the children the chance to focus on listening as a skill in its own right without it being attached to academic performance.

What format do you recommend for a group?

The format we use is six weekly sessions of around 30–50 minutes (depending upon the age of the class). The session is made up as follows:

- introduction or reinforcement of each of the four rules
- four activities to teach each of the four rules
- a final activity, which reinforces all of the rules
- summary of the rules and identification of times to use them in school.

A sample plan can be found in appendix 5.

We would recommend playing the games with children sitting on chairs as this is more conducive to good sitting but if the children spend any time in class sitting on the floor then you will need to spend at least one of the weeks practising the games while sitting on the floor. Don't forget to draw the children's attention to the fact that you are practising this because it is more difficult than sitting on a chair.

General ground rules when carrying out activities

All of the games have specified ground rules but these are the general rules that we work to:

- Not everyone has a turn during activities.
- Establish at the beginning the behaviour needed in order to get a turn. *These two rules prevent children switching off because they know they are going to get a turn anyway, and provides motivation for children to carry out the four rules so they can be chosen.*
- Be explicit to specific children in the group about why they are not getting chosen and explain what they need to do.
- During the session, give specific praise to children for good listening behaviour.

And finally … be explicit

- **Getting a turn**
  Our concern when we started playing these games with large groups was that not everyone would be able to have a turn. However, this has turned out to be the biggest advantage of a whole-class situation. The games are fun and everyone wants a turn but not everyone can have a turn. Only children who are showing good listening will get chosen and therefore the motivation to listen is very high. It is very important to be explicit with the children about what they will need to do to get a turn. If you can't give them a turn because they are not listening then explain this to them and remind them what the target is.
- **Sitting still while holding something**
  We have all encountered children who cannot have any object within arm's reach without fiddling with it and our instinct is often to move everything and create a desert around them. This can be a useful tactic but eventually in their school career they will have to listen while holding something. Some of the games involve the children holding an object or a picture and this is a useful chance to practise this skill. You will need explicitly to draw the children's attention to this as being a challenge. E.g. 'Did you know that it is very difficult to sit still while you are holding something? You might want to play with it or put it in your mouth but you can't – you've just got to keep still.' Then hand the objects/pictures out slowly, stopping every now and then to check whether the children are still doing a good job of sitting still even though they are holding something.
- **Staying quiet while moving**
  It appears to be a natural phenomenon of children everywhere that they talk when they walk! However quietly they were sitting to start with, asking them to stand up and move somewhere else will inevitably result in an outbreak of noise and chatter. The difficulty with this is, firstly, they stop listening to your instructions; secondly, it can take a while to refocus them back on the task in hand; and finally, a certain proportion of children will forget what they had to do anyway. Some of the games involve listening while moving and, again, it is worth drawing the children's attention to this particular challenge. E.g. 'When you stand up you will want to talk to your friends but I want to see if you can do this game really quietly because that will help you to keep listening.' Remind the children of times that they can practise this in class.
- **Making it harder**
  If you are going to play a harder version of a game, make sure you tell the children. There is something very motivating for the children in knowing this. E.g. 'We are going to play the sitting still game again next week but I'm going to make it MORE difficult!'

Framework for all game instructions

All the games are laid out in the following format:

Rule – Game Number	
Name of the Game	
How to play:	Description of the game.
Equipment:	What you will need to play.
To make it easier: **To make it harder:**	Suggestions for differentiating the game for different ages and abilities or to allow progression.
Ground Rules:	Basic rules which need to be established before you start, to make sure the game works as you mean it to.
Inside Information:	Extra information that we have learned from playing the games lots of times with lots of children.
Multi-rule	Multi-rule Game – lots of the games practise more than one skill but this section will point out any games which are equally useful for teaching another rule.
EY	Indicates a game which is particularly suitable for Early Years classes (5 years or below) or children who are functioning at this level.

5 Looking at the person who is talking

This is a good rule to teach first, as the games typically have a low level of language involvement. This means that even children with significant language or learning difficulties can participate.

The rule is 'Looking at the person who is talking' rather than just 'looking'. This is because children often learn to look at the teacher but then do not generalise this skill with other people. Our aim is for the children we work with to become good listeners in every situation whether this is learning to look at other children in group work or understanding that they need to look at the lunchtime supervisor when she is speaking to them on the playground. Consequently, games used to teach this rule must develop to involve looking at other children as well as the teacher or adult.

The games are all designed so that eye contact gets an immediate and tangible reward. The games have been developed to demonstrate to children that making eye contact with someone else enables them to find out information they would not have otherwise. This is very important if children are to see the point of eye contact and to generalise it as a skill in everyday life.

We have often been asked about the appropriateness and practicalities of using these games with children on the autistic spectrum. Almost every group we have run in school has had at least one child with an autistic spectrum type difficulty of varying severity. Our experience has been that these children have fallen into two categories with regard to eye contact. The first group of children are not distressed by eye contact but do not use it because they do not understand the point of it. This group of children respond really well to these games because the reward for eye contact is made much more explicit and they are consequently far more motivated to use it. The second, and smaller, group of children actively dislike eye contact and find it distressing. This group of children can still join in the games but it may be helpful to modify expectations on their looking and not ask them to make direct eye contact. Instead you can encourage them to look in the general direction of the person, perhaps focusing on their shoulder instead of their eyes. In our opinion, it is worth encouraging this, as looking at someone when they are talking is such a key social skill and influences how children are viewed by both teachers and other children.

Looking at the person who is talking – Game 1

Who looks different?

How to play:
One child puts on a blindfold. Another child in the group changes their appearance in some way. The first child has to take off the blindfold and look at all the children to see who looks different.

Equipment:
- Blindfold
- Selection of props – a mixture of obvious (Silly hats and glasses) and subtle (real glasses, necklaces. etc.). Try to select props which focus on the head and face as this is where we want to encourage children to look.

To make it easier:
- Use very obvious props – e.g. high-visibility jacket.
- Just use one prop and tell the child what they are looking for: 'Who's got the hat on?'

To make it harder:
- Use subtle props such as a real pair of glasses or a hair slide, etc.

Ground Rules:
- Everyone has to keep looking at the person who had the blindfold.

Inside Information:
- This sounds like a very easy game and it certainly can be played successfully with very young children. However, it is not as easy as it appears when it is played with a larger group and it is a good starting point to teaching looking with older children too.
- Always start with obvious props, whatever the age or the ability of the children. Silly props are more fun and help children to get the idea of looking at the rest of the group in a systematic way.

Looking at the person who is talking – Game 2

Who feels different?

How to play:
One child puts on a blindfold. Another child in the group is given an emotion picture. They have to hide the card behind their back and make the face on it. Everyone else has to make a happy face. The first child has to take off the blindfold and look at all the children's faces to see who feels different. If they have chosen correctly then the child produces the card from behind their back.

Equipment:
• Blindfold
• Emotion pictures – happy/cross/sad/surprised (appendix 6)

To make it easier:
• Tell the child which emotion card they are looking for: 'Who's got a cross face?'

To make it harder:
• Give out more than one emotion card. The child then has to find who feels and different **and** say how they feel.

TIP: Start by giving out just the 'cross' card as this appears to be easiest for children to recognise, then move on to giving out both the 'cross' card and the 'surprised' card. Finally, give out the 'cross', 'surprised' and 'sad' cards. This is the most difficult as children often find it hard to discriminate between 'cross' and 'sad'.

Ground Rules:
• Everyone has to keep looking at the person who had the blindfold.
• Everyone apart from the child who has the emotion card has to make a happy face.

Inside Information:
• Spend time practising making the faces, with a mirror if necessary.
• Play the game several times, introducing an extra emotion picture each time. Build up to hiding sad, cross and surprised faces.
• Don't let the child take the blindfold off until everyone else is making a happy face.
• Don't try to hide the happy face too – unless the other children have been given a specific face to make they will copy one of the children hiding an emotion card!

Emotion partners

How to play:
All of the children are given an emotion card. They are not allowed to show the card to anyone else. On the count of three, the children have to stand up, make their face and find someone else who feels the same as them.

Equipment:
• Emotion pictures – happy/cross/sad/surprised (appendix 6)

To make it easier:
• Just use two emotion cards.
• Ask the children to find just one other person with the same face.

To make it harder:
• Use all four emotion cards.
• Ask the children to find everyone with the same card as them.

Ground Rules:
• Everyone has to keep making their face.
• Don't show your card to anyone else!

Inside Information:
• Spend time practising making the faces, with a mirror if necessary.
• This game is useful for rearranging groups.
• With older children, introduce a competitive element by timing how long it takes for the class to divide into the four groups. Try to beat the class record each time.

Looking at the person who is talking – Game 4

Round and round Charlie goes

How to play:
One child hides their eyes or goes out of the room. The other children pass the teddy (or any other cuddly toy) around the group saying the rhyme:

'Round and round Charlie goes, where he stops nobody knows.' The child who is holding the teddy when the rhyme stops, hides it behind their back. All the other children have to put their hands behind their backs too. The child who has been hiding their eyes then has three chances to guess who has Charlie.

Equipment:
• Cuddly toy

To make it easier:
• The child can get up and look for Charlie around the circle.

Ground Rules:
• Everyone has to put their hands behind their backs.
• Everyone has to look at the child who has hidden their eyes.

Inside Information:
• Children must keep their hands behind their backs while the child is guessing.
• If a child is chosen then they can show their hands to demonstrate whether they have Charlie or not.

Multi-rule

This can be used as a keeping-still game with younger children. They have to keep their hands behind their backs until they are chosen.

Looking at the person who is talking – Game 5

The Blinking Game

How to play:
One child is the detective. This child has to go out of the room or hide their eyes. One of the other children is given the blinking picture. They must hide this behind their back and keep blinking their eyes. The detective then has to come in and find out which child is hiding the blinking picture.

Equipment:
• The blinking picture (appendix 7)

To make it easier:
• Walk with the child around the circle, encouraging them to look at each face and deciding whether that child has the card or not.

To make it harder:
• Play blink murder. The person with the blinking card has to blink at the other children. When they are blinked at the child must pretend to die. The detective has to find out who the 'murderer' is.

Ground Rules:
• Everyone has to look at the detective.
• Only the person who has the blinking card is allowed to keep blinking.

Inside Information:
• This is a good game for encouraging eye contact in a non-threatening and concrete way.
• Emphasise the rule that only the person with the blinking card is allowed to **keep** blinking.
• Explain that the other children can blink as they normally would but they can't **keep** blinking. You might need an adult to model the difference!

Looking at the person who is talking – Game 6

Looking Pairs

How to play:
A ball is placed in the centre of the circle. All the group members look at the ball and think of another person in the group. At the count of three, everyone looks at the person they were thinking of. If that person is looking at them too, they can swap seats.

Equipment:
- Ball

To make it easier:
- The children have to choose one of the adults to look at. This increases the chances of making a looking pair.

To make it harder:
- Add a language component – for example the children have to choose another child with the same colour hair as them.

Ground Rules:
- No talking!
- You are not allowed just to choose your friends.
- You must change who you are thinking of every turn.

Inside Information:
- This is a really good game for helping children to recognise eye contact.
- As this is a completely non-verbal game it is good game to use as an ice breaker or with children with poor language skills.
- Emphasise the 'no talking' rule or children will cheat by negotiating a partner in advance.

Who is the leader?

How to play:
One child is the detective. This child has to go out of the room or hide their eyes. One of the other children is given the leader picture. They must hide this and then start leading the actions, e.g. clapping, tapping, nodding, etc. The detective then has to come in and work out which child is the leader.

Equipment:
• Leader card (appendix 8)

To make it easier:
• Just play 'follow the leader'. The adult is the leader and the children have to watch and copy the actions.

Ground Rules:
• Everyone has to look at the leader.

Inside Information:
• This is a good game for encouraging children to look for eye contact between other people.
• Even if you are planning to play 'Who is the leader?' start with 'Follow the leader' because the children need lots of ideas for actions.
• Remember that once the detective is back in the room you will not be able to give the leader any more ideas for actions without giving the game away so make sure that your leader has plenty of ideas.

Pass the turn

How to play:
Select an activity or game which is appropriate to the age group. This could be building a tower, completing a puzzle, knocking down skittles or taking a turn in a commercial game. Select one person to be in charge of the turns. This person will pass the turn to other people in the group by looking at them and giving them a little nod.

Equipment:
• Game or activity

To make it easier:
• The adult has the turn and the children have to look at the adult if they want a turn.
• The next level of complexity would be to select a child to be in charge of the turns. Start with the child sitting in the adult's seat and progress to choosing children sitting in different places around the circle so that the children have to vary where they look.

To make it harder:
• Pass the turn around the circle. The first child passes the turn to the second child. Everyone then looks at the second child who passes the turn to a third child and so on. This is more difficult because the children in the group, firstly, have to give eye contact to a child rather than an adult and, secondly, have to keep changing the focus of their eye contact to different points around the circle.

Ground Rules:
• If you want a turn you must look at the leader.
• The leader ONLY chooses people who are looking at them, sitting still and staying quiet.
• If you carry on doing good looking you might get another turn.

Inside Information:
• You can play this game without an activity as long as the reward for looking is something motivating. For example, lining up at the door, going out to play, etc. This is a really good way to move children from one activity to another in a silent and orderly manner.
• This is a good game to practise lots of listening skills at the same time – looking, staying quiet and sitting still. It can be played lots of times without the children losing motivation as long as the activity is changed regularly.
• Make sure you set the ground rules in advance – 'If you want a turn, who do you need to look at? Am I going to chose anyone who is shouting out?', etc.
• Look out for someone who is still doing good looking even after they have had a go and give them another turn as soon as possible. This will stop children switching off when they have had a turn and motivate them to keep looking.

Multi-rule

This game can also be used to teach the 'Keeping quiet' rule as children do not get chosen unless they are staying quiet.

Looking at the person who is talking – Game 9

There's a space next to me …

How to play:
One extra chair is placed in the circle. The people sitting either side of the space have to put their hand on the chair as quickly as possible. The first person to touch the chair can choose someone to sit on it. They do this by looking around the circle and making eye contact with another person. That person moves to the chair, leaving a space behind and the game continues.

Equipment:
• None

To make it easier:
• If eye contact is hard – choose someone by nodding at them.

Ground Rules:
• You cannot touch the chair until the person has got up.
• If the space is next to you, you must choose people who are looking at you, sitting still and staying quiet.
• You can't just choose your friends.
• If you are a girl, you can't just choose girls and if you are a boy, you can't just choose boys.
• Keep on looking and you might get another turn.

Inside Information:
• Eye contact can be difficult for some children to use naturally. Try asking children to look at someone and give them a little nod. This often looks and feels more natural than eye contact alone.

Multi-rule

This game can also be used to teach the 'Keeping quiet' rule as children are not allowed to say anyone else's name – they have to chose someone just by looking.

Looking at the person who is talking – Game 10

Who is in the tunnel?

How to play:
Place a pop-up tunnel in the centre of the circle. One child goes out of the room. Another child in the group hides in the tunnel. The first child has to come back in and look around the circle and decide who is in the tunnel.

Equipment:
• Pop-up tunnel

To make it easier:
• Tell the child whether it is a boy or a girl hiding in the tunnel.

To make it harder:
• All the other children swap places to rearrange the group.

Ground Rules:
• Everyone has to keep looking at the person who has been out of the room.

Inside Information:
• You can play this game without a tunnel by just hiding the child somewhere else in the room.

6 Sitting still

Children who find it difficult to stay still often have very little insight into their own behaviour. When teaching this rule it is helpful to build in an element which gives children feedback into their sitting and shows them when they are carrying out the rule successfully.

It is important to practise these activities with children sitting on chairs **and** on the floor. Chairs are easier for children to sit still on, but as they spend time in school sitting on the floor too, they need opportunities to practise this rule in both situations.

When children first attempt to sit still without fidgeting, it can be a challenging task, which takes a lot of effort and concentration and does not always feel comfortable. However, the more children practise this rule the easier it becomes to do unconsciously.

It is sometimes recommended that children have an object that they can fidget with unobtrusively. This may be helpful for some children but it needs to be monitored carefully. In order for it to be a successful approach the child needs to have insight into his own fidgeting, and learn to do this without distracting himself or other children.

Sitting still – Game 1

Traffic light waiting

How to play:
Put the pop-up tunnel in the centre of the room. Stand next to the tunnel entrance with the stop/go sign turned to 'stop'. A child is chosen to go through the tunnel. However, they cannot go through straight away. They have to wait until you turn the sign to 'go'.

Equipment:
• Stop/go sign (appendix 9)
• Pop-up tunnel

To make it easier:
• Only wait a second or two before turning the sign around.

To make it harder:
• Increase the amount of time that the child has to wait before they get the 'go' sign.

Ground Rules:
• Only children who are sitting still and not shouting out will get chosen to have a turn in the tunnel.
• Only one child is allowed to go through the tunnel at a time. Everyone else must stay sitting still.

Inside Information:
• This is a really good game to teach children to wait for a turn. It is a good starting point for children who are very active or impulsive.
• Other activities can be used instead of a tunnel but this seems to be effective as it is very motivating, particularly for the very active children that the game targets.
• It helps to focus the child if you count out loud before turning the sign round: 'You got to three last time – how long can you wait this time? One … two … three …'
• Always start with a very short wait and work upwards, however easy it seems. This ensures the children experience success. For some impulsive children, delaying what they want to do for even 5 seconds is a real achievement.
• If you are familiar with a signing system then using the sign and saying 'wait' can help to focus the child.

Sitting still – Game 2
Musical mats

How to play:
Put five mats in the centre of the room and choose five children to walk or dance around to the music. When the music stops the children must go and sit on their mats until the music starts again.

Equipment:
• Mats or chairs
• Music

To make it easier:
• Use chairs instead of mats.
• Make the intervals between the music shorter.

To make it harder:
• Increase the intervals between the music so that children have to sit still for longer.
• Children have to stand on the mats instead of sitting. This is harder because it is much easier for impulsive children to run off.

Ground Rules:
• You must stay on the chair/mat until the music starts again.

Inside Information:
• This is a really good game to teach young children to manage their impulsive behaviour and wait for an adult cue. It is a good starting point for children who can't stay on a chair because it starts by requiring them to wait for just a second or two and builds on this.
• Again, it really helps to focus the child if the adult counts out loud before turning the music back on: 'ready? One … two … three … four … off we go again.'
• Don't start counting straight away. Take a moment to make sure the children are all on their chairs or mats.
• Always start with a very short interval and work on lengthening this. Being able to count up to approximately 15 is a good result.
• If the adult is familiar with a signing system then using the sign and saying 'wait' really helps to focus the child.
• This game is about children learning to stay on a chair. It is not about perfect sitting – there are other games in this section which deal with this. Some fidgeting is therefore allowed but children MUST stay on their chair or mat.

Sitting still – Game 3

Sitting still with instruments

How to play:

Begin by telling the children that it is very hard to sit still when holding a musical instrument because if you fidget the instrument will make a noise and everyone will be able to hear that you are fidgeting. Then tell the children that you are going to give everyone an instrument and they must hold it really still. Then hand out an instrument to each child, stopping every three or four children to listen to see whether everyone is still doing a good job of sitting still.

When everyone has an instrument they must keep it still for a given period. We use a pecking bird on a stick which takes about 15 seconds to go from top to bottom but it would be possible to use a rainmaker or a timer or another suitable toy. When the pecking bird reaches the bottom, everyone can play their instruments until you say 'stop'.

Equipment:
• A musical instrument for each child
• A pecking bird, rainmaker or timer

To make it easier:
• Choose instruments which are easy to keep quiet, e.g. castanets.

To make it harder:
• Increase the amount of time the children have to wait before playing.
• When the pecking bird has finished, point to just one child. They can play their instrument but everyone else has to carry on keeping still. This is more difficult as it requires a greater degree of self control.
• Choose a child to be the leader. They are in charge of the timer and choose which child plays the instrument when it stops.

Ground Rules:
• Putting your instrument on the floor is cheating! The children must hold the instrument and keep it still.
• The grown up chooses which instrument each child has.

Inside Information:
• Unless all of the instruments are identical, the children will want to start a debate about which instrument they are going to have. To stop the activity descending into chaos it must be established that it is the adult who chooses!
• If you know that a child within the group will find this particularly challenging then make sure they have an instrument which is easy to keep quiet, e.g. castanets.
• If a child is deliberately sabotaging the game by making a noise then give them one warning 'I can't play this game if you are making a noise … can you keep it still?' and then remove the instrument if they continue to be disruptive.

Sitting still – Game 4

What am I doing wrong?

How to play:
Sit on a chair in the middle of the room and say 'I'm going to do some things now which are NOT good sitting. Put your hand up if you know what they are.' Then model as many types of fidgeting behaviour as possible. The children put up their hands to identify behaviour and you respond with, for example 'You're right. I'm rocking on my chair. Can you still do good sitting while you are rocking on your chair?'

Equipment:
• None needed but it helps, and makes it more fun, if you have items that the children usually fidget with, for example, shoes with Velcro on them, a tie, a hair band, etc.

Ground Rules:
• If you see the grown-up doing something which is NOT good sitting then you must put your hand up. You cannot shout out.

Inside Information:
• This activity is an essential precursor to any of the further activities which target fidgeting. In our experience, children have very little insight into their own sitting and this activity both raises their awareness of what fidgeting is and establishes the principle that you cannot do good listening while you are fidgeting.
• It is really important to model all the fidgeting behaviours that you want to target in the children you are working with. Do not expect children to generalise the term 'fidgeting' to whatever behaviour it is that they do without having their attention explicitly drawn to it. Obviously, the names of specific children do not need to be mentioned.
• Some fidgeting behaviours that you might want to model are:

  ➢ rocking on chair
  ➢ playing with Velcro on shoes
  ➢ taking shoes off
  ➢ playing with hair
  ➢ sucking thumb
  ➢ chewing cuff
  ➢ rolling down socks
  ➢ messing with other children

And if you are brave enough:

  ➢ nose picking
  ➢ putting hands down trousers!

The children you work with will almost certainly inspire many more.

Sitting still – Game 5

Fidget monitor

How to play:
One child is chosen to be the fidget monitor and puts on the fidget monitor badge (appendix 10). They go out of the room, with an adult if possible. While they are out of the room another child is chosen to have the fidget card (appendix 10). The fidget sits on the card to hide it and chooses something to do which is NOT good sitting. Everyone else has to do their very best sitting. The fidget monitor comes back in, looks carefully at how everyone is sitting and works out who has the fidget card.

Equipment:
• Fidget monitor badge (appendix 10)
• Fidget card (appendix 10)

To make it easier:
• The adult walks with the child and helps them to look at each child one at a time – asking 'Are they doing good sitting?'
• Use very obvious fidgeting.

To make it harder:
• Use very subtle fidgeting – but have lots of practice with more obvious fidgeting to make sure that the group are good at sitting before trying this.

Ground Rules:
• Everyone has to keep looking at the fidget monitor.
• Everyone else has to keep doing their best sitting.

Inside Information:
• Always play 'What am I doing wrong?' before attempting this game as this teaches children what fidgeting is.
• Any teacher will be able to predict what will happen the first time you play this game – the fidget monitor will pick out 4 or 5 children who are fidgeting and DO NOT have the fidget card. These children are usually very indignant because they had no idea that they were not sitting well. This gives the adult the opportunity to say 'Oh we thought that you had the fidget card because you were … can you show me good sitting?' For this reason this is a really good activity for raising children's awareness of their own sitting and by the second time of playing it children are usually trying very hard to sit still.
• When the fidget monitor has gone out, the adult in the room needs to focus specific children on the target behaviour – e.g. 'Do you remember? Last time the fidget monitor thought you had the card because you were chewing your jumper so you've got to remember to sit really still.' Then remember to give them lots of praise if they manage this.
• The adult who has gone out with the fidget monitor should remind them what they need to do – 'We're going to look at everyone and see if anybody is doing anything which is NOT good sitting.'

Sitting still – Game 6

Sitting still with timer

How to play:
Put five mats in the centre of the room. Choose one child to be the leader and four other children. The children line up behind leader. When the stop/go sign is turned to 'go' the children walk around the mats until the 'stop' sign is shown. Then the children sit on the mats. The children have to do their very best sitting and not fidget. Everyone else has to watch them and put their hand up if they see anyone fidgeting. When everyone is settled, the timer is started. As soon as someone moves the timer is stopped and the children sit down. The next group of children try to beat the score.

Equipment:
• Mats or chairs
• Timer
• Stop/go sign (appendix 9)

To make it easier:
• If you have a child who is likely to find this very difficult, then an adult can sit opposite them on the floor. This keeps them focused and blocks out some of the distractions.
• Use chairs.

To make it harder:
• See game 7.

Ground Rules:
• The children who are watching must put their hands up – they cannot shout out.
• The grown-ups make the final decision whether someone has fidgeted.
• The children are allowed to breathe and blink!

Inside Information:
• This sounds a very dull game but the children love it. Even the children who are watching are motivated as they want to catch the other children out.
• Wait until everyone is settled before starting the timer. This gives children time to find a comfortable sitting position.
• Aim for a maximum of 75–90 seconds. If children reach this, stop the timer and tell them how well they have done.
• Start with children that you know can sit well and then target the poor sitters.
• It is important to establish the ground rule that you can breathe, blink and smile and still do good sitting or you will get a lot of false reports of fidgeting!
• A powerful part of this game is the fact that the child knows that you have seen them do really good sitting. Make the link for them with other situations in which they can practise this – 'I am so proud of you! Can you do that really good sitting at carpet time?'

Sitting still – Game 7

Sitting still with distractions

How to play:
This is a game to help children practise sitting still even when someone next to them is being silly and trying to distract them. Explain that you are going to play the 'Sitting still' game (see game 6) but that this time it is going to be MORE difficult because when they are sitting on the mat you are going to do something which makes it much harder for them to keep sitting still. 'I'm going to blow bubbles and they might land on your hair … they might land on your nose … they might land right next to you but you CAN'T pop them and you CAN'T fidget. You've just got to keep sitting still.' Then play the game exactly as before with the added distraction of bubbles and stop the timer when someone fidgets.

Equipment:
- Mats or chairs
- Timer
- Stop/go sign (appendix 9)
- Bubbles
- Other distractions such as feather dusters, mini fans, etc

To make it easier:
- See game 6

To make it harder:
- Use other distractions such as feather dusters to tickle them or mini fans to blow their hair etc.

Ground Rules:
- The children who are watching must put their hands up – they cannot shout out.
- The grown-ups decide if someone has fidgeted.
- The children are allowed to breathe and blink!

Inside Information:
- Start with 'Sometimes when children are trying to sit really well, someone next to them is a bit silly and talks to them or messes with their hair or clothes. Does that ever happen to you?' Explain that this game is to help them practise doing good sitting even when someone next to them is being really silly.
- Make the link for the children – 'I can't believe that you sat still for a whole minute even though I was blowing bubbles on you! Now I know that you can do really good sitting on the carpet even if the other children are being silly.'
- Praise children in the general group if you see them trying to ignore a child who is attempting to distract them. This is a more powerful way of tackling this behaviour within the group than telling off the child who is being silly.

Sitting still – Game 8

Pass the squeeze

How to play:
All of the children and adults sit in a circle and hold hands. Everyone but the leading adult closes their eyes. The leader starts the squeeze by squeezing the hand of one of the children next to them. That child will them pass the squeeze on the next child and so on round the circle. You can only squeeze the hand of the next person once you have received the squeeze yourself. The aim is to get the squeeze back to the leader.

Equipment:
• None

To make it easier:
• Just pick a few children to make a small circle.
• Do the activity with eyes open so children can watch where the squeeze is.

To make it harder:
• Keep where the squeeze is going to start a secret and, when all the children have their eyes shut, pat a child on the head to start the squeeze.

Ground Rules:
• Everyone needs to keep their eyes shut.
• Be explicit that you can only squeeze when it's your go.

Inside Information:
• Explain to the children that they need to keep really still, otherwise they will not feel the person squeezing their hand.
• Children who are uncomfortable when others invade their personal space may find this a difficult game.

Sitting still – Game 9

The parachute game

How to play:
Put the parachute in the centre of the room and choose a number of children to sit in a circle and hold the edges of the parachute. Put the noisy ball in the centre of the parachute and, once it is still, start the timer. As soon as the ball moves and makes a noise the timer is stopped. The next group of children try to beat the score.

Equipment:
- Small parachute or circular tablecloth
- Noise-making ball
- Timer

To make it easier:
- Children sit on chairs.

To make it harder:
- Children sit on the floor.
- The adult chooses a child to let go of the parachute and the rest of the group have to keep the ball still.
- Use a large parachute that the whole class can hold and see if they can beat their previous score.

Ground Rules:
- You can't let go of the parachute unless a grown-up tells you to.

Inside Information:
- Introduce the game by saying 'This game helps everyone to do good sitting but we all need to work together.'
- This is a challenging game and may be more suitable for older children as they need to work as a team in order to be successful.

Sitting still – Game 10

Pass the hat

How to play:
For this game you will need two teams. Team 1 will be 'hat wearers' and team 2 will be 'hat passers'. Go round the circle putting every other child in team 1. Then give a hat to a child in team 2. This child has to put a hat on the team 1 child next to them. Then the next team 2 child will move it to the next team 1 child and so on. The aim is for the hat to be passed on to the head of every other child in the circle but they must sit still while this is happening. If someone fidgets or touches the hat while they are wearing it, say 'stop' and see how far the hat has travelled round the circle. You will then need to change over the teams so that team 2 are wearing the hat. Their challenge is to see if they can move the hat further round the circle than team 1 did. The ultimate aim is for the hat to travel all the way round the circle with each child who has to wear it managing to sit still.

Equipment:
• Hat

To make it harder:
• Have two hats travelling round starting at opposite ends of the circle.

Ground Rules:
• The hat wearers must keep sitting still.
• The hat passers must put the hats on the children next to them gently.

Inside Information:
• This is a game to help children practise sitting still even if other children next to them are trying to be distracting.
• You need to use hats that are too big for children (i.e. easy to put on and take off) and with no scratchy headbands or chin straps that could hurt children or catch their hair.
• It is worth modelling how to put the hat on other children's heads (and how not to!).

7 Staying quiet

The longer we have worked with children, the more obvious it has become that children who cannot stay quiet have a bigger impact on the listening environment than anything else. Furthermore, these children do not only disrupt their own listening, they distract other children and the adult who is trying to lead the activity. Children who fidget can be distracting but it is possible to ignore their behaviour in a way that is just not possible with children who shout out.

There are several different behaviours which children who find this rule challenging tend to exhibit:

- Some children can shout out comments that are totally irrelevant to the lesson, e.g. 'Tom is coming to my house for tea tonight!' Although this can be very disruptive, it is the easiest type of behaviour to deal with as it is obvious that what they are saying is unconnected to the activity and most adults would feel comfortable in pointing this out and refocusing the child on the topic.
- A more challenging group are children who shout out answers or comments that are relevant to the topic but do not put their hands up or wait to be chosen. Sometimes these children can be quite able and they may not have been identified as having listening difficulties. These are difficult children because for an adult leading an activity it is often actually quite encouraging to have a child who is engaged by the topic and wanting to volunteer answers. However, when they shout out they are disrupting the processing of other children who may have got to the answer if they had been given the time. In addition to this, learning to wait for your turn before speaking is an essential social skill which children need to develop to be successful communicators.
- A less common group of children are those who make non-verbal noises such as humming or tapping. These are less obviously intrusive than the children who shout out but tend to generate a continuous low-level noise which can be very distracting to anyone sitting near them.

These are all different difficulties but the common factor in all children who find it hard to stay quiet tends to be a lack of insight into their own behaviour. Consequently, the first step in teaching this rule is to raise children's awareness of when they are shouting out. They also need to have an opportunity to practise being quiet. The activities in this section will give children the chance to experience being quiet but it is equally important to be explicit about only choosing children who are being quiet and not shouting out. For all of these games it is important to praise the children for staying quiet and to make links for them to other situations where staying quiet will help everyone to listen. If you can improve children's performance on this rule it will make a huge impact on the listening and learning environment.

Staying quiet – Game 1

Sound location – boxes

How to play:
One child puts on a blindfold or goes out of the room. A musical toy or radio is hidden under one of the boxes. The child then takes off the blindfold and then has to listen to find which box the noise is coming from.

Explain the game to the children and then ask the group 'What can we do to help them do really good listening?' Hopefully, someone in the group will suggest being quiet. When they do you need to reinforce this. E.g. 'What a good idea! If we are really quiet then that will help them to do really good listening. If we are noisy they won't be able to hear that little noise.' Then play the game.

Equipment:
• Musical toy/radio
• 3 boxes
• Blindfold (if needed)

To make it easier:
• Use a really noisy toy or a radio with the volume turned up.
• Put the boxes far apart.

To make it harder:
• Use a very quiet toy or use a radio tuned to speech on low volume.
• Put the boxes close together

Ground Rules:
• Everyone has to stay quiet.
• Everyone has to look at the person with the blindfold.
• You must listen to all the boxes before you decide which one to turn over.

Inside Information:
• You MUST get an adult to model this activity first. Children always want to solve these tasks visually and will just lift up boxes to look unless an adult models actually getting down and listening.
• In addition to practising keeping quiet, this game is also a sound localisation game. This is an important skill for the classroom and conversation generally, so that children can hear a voice and know where to look.

Multi-rule

This game can be used as a 'listening' game for very young children who are not yet at the level of listening for words.

Staying quiet – Game 2

Sound location around the room

How to play:
One child goes out of the room. A musical toy or radio is hidden somewhere in room. The child then comes back into the room and then has to listen and find the noise maker.

Explain the game to the children and then ask the group 'What can we do to help them do really good listening?' Hopefully, someone in the group will suggest being quiet. When they do you need to reinforce this. E.g. 'What a good idea! If we are really quiet then that will help them to do really good listening. If we are noisy they won't be able to hear that little noise.' Then play the game.

Equipment:
• Noise maker or radio

To make it easier:
• Use a really noisy toy or a radio with the volume turned up.
• Tune the radio to music.

To make it harder:
• Use a very quiet toy or a radio on low volume.
• Tune the radio to speech.
• Hide a toy which makes a funny noise. This will make the children want to laugh so they will need to exert self-control to stay quiet. This is what we want children to do when listening in class.

Ground Rules:
• Everyone has to stay quiet.
• Everyone has to look at the person trying to find the toy.
• You must stop and listen before trying to find the noise maker

Inside Information:
• Again, children will want to solve this task visually and will tend to race around the room at top speed just looking for the noise maker. You must model standing in the middle of the room and listening first.
• You must establish the ground rule 'Everyone has to look at the person trying to find the toy' or children will look at the hidden noise maker and give the game away. If you know you have children within the group who will find it hard not to look at the toy, then give them this as a challenge: 'Do you know, I really want to put this radio behind your chair but I'm a bit worried that you will turn around and look at it and spoil the game. Can I trust you to be really sensible and just look at the person with the blindfold?' Then give them lots of praise when they do this. In our experience, children will always rise to a challenge given like this.
• Look out for other noise making items that you can hide, e.g. toys that talk; toys that make intermittent noises; etc.

Multi-rule

This game can be used as a 'listening' game for very young children who are not yet at the level of listening for words.

Staying quiet – Game 3
Giant's keys

How to play:
Put a chair in the centre of the room. On the floor behind the chair you need to put a box containing a big bunch of keys. One child is chosen to be the giant. They sit on the chair, put on a blindfold and pretend to go to sleep. Then point to another member of the group. That child is the thief and has to try to steal the keys and get back to their chair without waking the giant. If the giant hears any noise, they must point. If they point to the thief, then that child is out and you must choose a new giant and thief and try again.

Explain the game to the children and then ask them 'What can we do to help the giant do really good listening and catch the thief?' Point out to the children that if they stay really quiet it will help the giant to listen.

Equipment:
• Box
• Bunch of keys
• Blindfold

To make it easier:
• Do not put the keys in a box.
• Use a single key instead of a bunch.
• Ask the thief to jingle the keys when they get back to their seat so the giant can point to them.

To make it harder:
• Use a box with a catch that has to be opened.
• Use 'treasure' (assorted jewellery) instead of keys as this is harder to move without making a noise.

Ground Rules:
• Everyone has to stay really quiet.
• The giant cannot point until he has heard a noise.

Inside Information:
• You will need to have an adult model the giant's role first to show that the giant can only point when he hears a sound. This will help to prevent children pointing just to catch 'the thief'.
• Although you need to emphasise to the children that they must stay quiet, the children are usually already motivated to do this as they desperately want the giant to catch the thief out so they can have a turn!
• You will need to draw children's attention to how quiet they have been and make links with other situations in which the children need to keep that quiet. E.g. 'If you stay that quiet at carpet time then that will help everyone to do good listening.'

Staying quiet – Game 4

Silent treasure hunt

How to play:
One child goes out of the room. Then a box with 'treasure' in it is hidden in the room. The child comes back in the room and has to find the treasure. The other children cannot tell the child where the treasure is but they can help them find the treasure by looking at where it is hidden.

Equipment:
• Treasure box

To make it harder:
• Just select one person to look at the treasure. Everyone else has to look at the treasure hunter.

Ground Rules:
• Everyone has to stay really quiet.
• You can only use your eyes to give a clue about where to look – you are not allowed to point.

Inside Information:
• Remind the children to keep looking at the treasure even if the seeker is going somewhere else in the room.

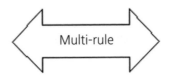
Multi-rule

This game can be used as a 'looking' game as children have to look at the treasure, and the treasure hunter has to work out where the treasure is by looking at their direction of gaze.

Staying quiet – Game 5

Secret messages

How to play:
Tell the children that you are going to play a game where you pass on messages but you are not allowed to talk. You have to use your face and hands to pass on the message. One child goes out of the room with an adult and practises a secret message. Then they come back into the room and do their mime without talking. The other children have to guess what the secret message is.

Equipment:
• Secret messages (appendix 11)

To make it easier:
• Choose the simple messages from the set.

Ground Rules:
• You must pass on the secret message without talking.

Inside Information:
• Children love this game but often find it difficult. Unless you are very confident that the children will be able to think of a mime, then you will need an adult to go out with the child and help them think of a way to convey their secret message. Generally children tend to be very poor at thinking of mimes and even worse at modifying them when people do not guess what it is!
• If the other children really cannot guess the message, then the child should go out of the room with an adult and decide how to modify the mime.

Staying quiet – Game 6

Who? What? Where?

How to play:
One child puts on a blindfold and sits on a chair in the middle of the room. Another child is chosen to stand somewhere in the room and play an instrument. The child with the blindfold has to guess who it is, say what instrument or noise it is and point to where the noise is coming from. Everyone has to stay really quiet so that the child with the blindfold can listen well.

Equipment:
• A selection of noise makers/instruments

To make it easier:
• Reduce the number of questions to just one or two, for example the child only has to point to where the noise is, or to point to the noise and say what noise it is.

To make it harder:
• Choose instruments which sound similar, e.g. bells and tambourine

Ground Rules:
• Everyone has to keep looking at the person with the blindfold.

Inside Information:
• You can use instruments for this game but it is fun to look for other noise makers, e.g. toys that make a noise when dropped; animals or birds which make a noise.

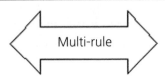
Multi-rule

This game can be used as a 'listening' game for very young children who are not yet at the level of listening for words.

Staying quiet – Game 7

What am I?

How to play:
This activity aims to stop children shouting out. Read clues one at a time from the 'What am I?' cards. Children are only allowed to guess if they are holding the talking ball and they must put their hand up to request the talking ball. The person who guesses correctly wins the card.

Equipment:
- Set of 'What am I?' cards (appendix 12)
- Ball

To make it easier:
- Use the easier set of 'What am I?' cards

To make it harder:
- Everyone has three lives. Every time you shout out you lose a life. If you lose all three lives you are out of the game.

Ground Rules:
- You can only talk if you are holding the talking ball.
- If you want to make a guess, put your hand up and wait for the adult to give you the ball.

Inside Information:
- This is a really good game to play with children who tend to shout out answers.
- Before you start the game remind children that if they want to talk they must put their hand up and wait for the ball.
- You must not give the talking ball to a child who has shouted out. If a child shouts out then say something like 'Oh – that's a shame. I really wanted to give you the ball but I can't when you shout out. Can you remember what I want you to do?'
- When a child who tends to shout out remembers to put their hand, try to give them a turn quickly to reinforce this and say 'Well done! Why could I give you a turn then?' They will usually be able to tell you that it is because they were quiet.

Staying quiet – Game 8

Keys around the circle

How to play:
This is an adaption of 'The giant's keys'. A child is chosen to be the giant. They sit on a chair in the middle of the circle, put on a blindfold and pretend to go to sleep. An empty box is placed behind them. Then the group have to pass the bunch of keys all the way around the circle without the giant hearing. The last person in the circle then has to put the keys back into the box, again without waking the giant.

If the giant hears a noise then he must point to where he heard the noise. If he points to the right place then the giant has won.

Equipment:
• Bunch of keys
• Box
• Blindfold

To make it easier:
• A big label attached to the keys makes it easier to pass on silently.
• Less jangly keys are easier to pass on silently.

To make it harder:
• The keys have to be put back in a box with a lid which will need to be opened.

Ground Rules:
• Everyone has to keep really quiet.
• The giant can only point when he hears a noise.

Inside Information:
• Before you play this game, you will need to spend some time talking about and demonstrating the best way to hand on the keys so that the giant doesn't hear.

Staying quiet – Game 9

Everyone gets a go

How to play:
The aim of this game is for everyone to have a turn at holding an object but the turn is given in silence by looking at the person and nodding at them. The children sit in a circle. Choose an object which is going to be passed and say 'Everyone is going to have a turn to hold the ball but we are not going to say anyone's name. When you need to pass the turn, you have got to look at a person and nod at them. If someone nods at you, you can get up very quietly and collect the ball and sit back down. Then it's your turn to choose someone else who hasn't had a turn yet.'

Equipment:
• Ball or other object

To make it easier:
• Put a sticker on each child who has already had a turn.

To make it harder:
• Use an object which is very hard to keep still, e.g. a bunch of keys.

Ground Rules:
• Everyone has to keep looking at the person who has the ball.
• Everyone has to stay really quiet, even when they get up to collect the ball.

Inside Information:
• This is a really good game to help children practise staying quiet when they move around the classroom. When you introduce the game say 'Sometimes children can stay really quiet when they are sitting still but when they have to move around the room they start talking. This game helps you to practise staying quiet even when you have to move.'

Multi-rule

This game can be used as a 'looking' game as the turn is passed on by looking and nodding at someone else.

Staying quiet – Game 10

How many children on the rug?

How to play:
Put a chair in the circle with a rug behind it. An adult sits on the chair and puts on a blindfold. Choose one half of the circle to go first. The object of the game is for children to get from their place in the circle onto the rug without making a noise. Children can only move onto the rug when you have tapped them on the head. If the adult hears anyone moving, they say 'stop' and that turn is then finished. The second half of the circle then have a turn. The winning team is the one which gets the most children onto the rug without making a noise.

Equipment:
• Rug
• Blindfold
• Timer (if needed)

To make it easier:
• Move the rug further away from the chair so that it is harder for the adult to hear any sounds.

To make it harder:
• Introduce a time constraint so that each team only has 30 seconds to get as many children as possible onto the rug. If the adult says 'stop' their time is over.

Ground Rules:
• Everyone has to stay quiet, including the half of the class who are not participating during a turn.
• You can only move when the adult touches your head.

Inside Information:
• You will need an adult to sit on the chair and listen, as children might find it difficult to distinguish between sounds in the room and the sounds of children moving onto the rug.
• Try to give each team more than one turn so that they get the chance to beat their score.
• This is a good game to help children practise moving around the classroom quietly. When you introduce the game say 'Sometimes children can stay really quiet when they are sitting still but when they have to move around the room they start talking. This game helps you to practise staying quiet even when you have to move.'

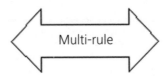
Multi-rule

This game can also be used as a 'keeping still' game as children must keep really still on the rug to avoid making a noise.

8 Listening to all the words

There are several different reasons why children can fail to listen to all of the words in an instruction:

- Some children appear to need instructions to be directed specifically at them and do not follow instructions given to the whole class. They may only listen if their name is called.
- Other children may listen to the first part of an instruction, recognise the scenario and think they know what is coming next, and then stop listening. It is often relatively able children who do this but they are caught out when the instruction is different from the one they predicted.
- With a familiar activity, children may not listen at all as they have already experienced the task and think they know the routine. As classrooms are often quite predictable environments, this can be a successful strategy some of the time. Of course, a problem occurs when they are being asked to do something new or different.
- An instruction may contain a 'trigger phrase' such as 'Line up at the door,' or 'It's nearly dinnertime.' When children hear a phrase like this, it is often the end of any attempt at listening and they don't pay attention to anything else in the instruction.
- Classrooms are often very 'fair' places where everyone has a turn to speak or to do an activity. However, many children will switch off once they have had a turn as they know they don't have to listen any more.

The activities in this section put children in situations where they have to listen to **all** of the words in order successfully to carry out the task. However, as listening to words inevitably means some language involvement, these activities can be challenging for either very young children or those with language or learning difficulties. For this reason the first games in this section involve listening to musical instruments or just single words so that this rule can be practised with children who have limited verbal skills.

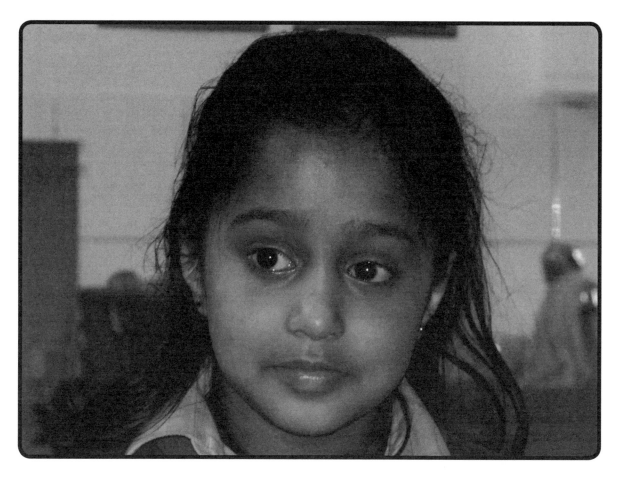

Listening to all the words – Game 1

Matching musical instruments

How to play:
Put one set of instruments in front of the child. The other set should be kept in the bag. You play one of the instruments in the bag and the child has to select and play the one that matches. Then take the instrument out of the bag to show the child that they are the same.

Equipment:
• Two matching sets of 3 or 4 instruments
• A bag or other barrier

To make it easier:
• Just have a choice of two instruments.

To make it harder:
• Increase the numbers of instruments the child has to choose from.
• Use similar sounding instruments.
• Play a sequence of 2 or more instruments. The child then has to select the right instruments AND put them in the right order. **TIP:** This is also a really good early literacy activity.

Ground Rules:
• Listen to the sound BEFORE you touch the instruments.

Inside Information:
• If a child finds it really difficult to match the instruments using sound alone, start by taking the instrument out of the bag before playing it so that it becomes a visual matching activity. Draw the child's attention to the sound and when the child is confident at this, try again with just the sound.
• The children will certainly want to play the instruments and it is probably wise to let them get this out of their system first! With a small group, pass each instrument around so each child can play it once before the activity. With a large group, let the child have a quick chance to play the instruments before their turn.

Listening for 'go'

How to play:
You will need a marble run or similar activity. The activity needs to be very motivating. The child is given the marble but cannot put it down the marble run until you say 'go'.

Equipment:
• A marble run or equivalent

To make it easier:
• Only wait a second or two before saying 'go'.
• Say 'Ready … steady … GO!' to keep the child focused.
• Use the stop/go sign to help focus the child

To make it harder:
• Increase the amount of time that the child has to wait before you say 'go'.
• Whisper 'go' but warn the child that you are going to make it harder and they will have to listen very carefully.

Ground Rules:
• Only children who are sitting still and not shouting out will get chosen to have a turn with the marble run.
• You MUST wait to hear 'go' before you put the marble down the run.

Inside Information:
• As well as being a good listening game, this is a good activity to teach children to wait for an adult signal. It is a good starting point for managing the behaviour of children who are very active or impulsive.
• It may help to focus the child if you count out loud before saying 'go' – 'You got to 5 last time – how long can you wait this time? One … two … three …'
• Always start with a very short wait and work upwards, however easy it seems to ensure the children experience success.
• If you are familiar with a signing system then using the sign and saying 'wait' can help to focus the child.

Listening to all the words – Game 3

Listening for your name

How to play:
The children sit in a circle. Blow bubbles in the middle of the circle and then say a name of one of the children in the group. That child can get up and burst the bubbles. Everyone else has to stay on their seats.

Equipment:
- Bubbles

To make it easier:
- Point to the child at the same time as you say their name.

Ground Rules:
- Only the person whose name is called can get off their chair.
- Only the person whose name is called can burst the bubbles.
- Only children who are sitting still and staying quiet will have their name called.
- Even if you have had a turn, if you keep sitting still and staying quiet, your name might get called again.

Inside Information:
- Another activity could be used but we have not found anything more motivating, for such a wide age range, than bursting bubbles!
- Although this is a listening game, it is a really good game for teaching self-restraint. All the children want to burst the bubbles but only one can and you can only have a turn if you are sitting still and staying quiet. Consequently, it really motivates children to listen well.

Multi-rule

This game can also be used as a 'keeping still' game for young children as, despite the temptation of the bubbles, the children have to stay on their chair.

Fruit salad

How to play:
Each child is given a picture of a fruit. Say the names of two fruits. Any children holding those fruits must stand up and swap chairs. If you say 'fruit salad' then everyone can swap chairs.

In the traditional version of this game, children are just told which fruit they are. The difficulty with this is that children either cannot remember what fruit they are or they decide that they don't like bananas and would prefer to be a plum. Giving them a picture of the fruit stops this issue and also helps them to practise sitting still whilst holding something which is a very important skill for school.

Equipment:
• Pictures of fruit

To make it easier:
• Go slowly and make sure everyone is sitting down and focused before saying the next fruits.

To make it harder:
• You can make it harder for individual children by not saying their fruit for a while and then saying it two or three times in a row. This catches out children who tend to switch off once they have had a turn.

Ground Rules:
• You must keep your picture still.
• You must stay quiet while you are moving to a new chair.
• You must walk to the new chair.

Inside Information:
• Before you give out the pictures say to the children 'It's very hard to sit still while you are holding something. When I give you the card you might want to flick it or chew it but you can't. You've got to keep it still.' Every few children, stop and check how everyone is doing with holding the pictures still.
• In school, children are often very noisy when moving from one activity to another. Tell the children that this game will help them to practise moving and staying quiet. They cannot talk when moving to a new chair or they will not hear which fruit is next.
• This is a really good game for children who tend to copy the child next to them. Make sure that you mix the pictures up so that children cannot copy.
• You do not have to say 'Fruit salad'. If you feel the group is too lively, then do NOT say it!
• You can use any topic pictures, e.g. clothes – 'washing machine'; transport – 'traffic jam'; or you could choose pictures relevant to the class topic.

Multi-rule

This game can be used as a 'keeping still' game as children have to practise holding their picture still. It can also be used as a 'keeping quiet' game as they have to practise getting up and moving without talking.

Listening to all the words – Game 5

Talking ball – semantic categories

How to play:
The children sit in a circle. Pick a topic, e.g. animals, and pass the ball from child to child. Each child has to say something from the topic but they cannot say the same as anyone else.

Equipment:
• Ball

To make it easier:
• Children who are shy or have language problems may have difficulty thinking of something to say. In this situation, it is helpful to use 'phone-a-friend' which means they can select another child in the group to help them out.

To make it harder:
• Instead of just passing the ball round, YOU have control of where the ball goes. Tell the children 'You MUST keep listening because I might come back to you.' Then hand the ball to random members of the group, repeatedly going back to any children who tend to switch off.

Ground Rules:
• You can only talk when you are holding the ball.

Inside Information:
• This is intended to be a listening activity not a language activity and so you will need to minimise the stress on children who might have language difficulties. You can use 'phone-a-friend' as described above but also try to place children who might find this task a challenge near the beginning of the circle.
• This is a really good game to help children listen to each other instead of just listening to the teacher. Remind the children of this – 'Who do you have to listen to to be good at this game? – everyone.'
• Playing the harder version radically improves children's listening as they do not know if the ball is coming back to them or not, but you must raise their awareness of this before you play so they know that they have got to keep listening.
• Suitable topics might be:

  ➢ animals
  ➢ colours
  ➢ food
  ➢ people who help us
  ➢ subjects in school

Listening to all the words – Game 6

Pass the object

How to play:
The children sit in a circle. Choose an interesting object related to a current topic and pass it from child to child. Each child has to say something about the object, such as what it feels like or where it comes from, but they cannot say the same thing as anyone else. See how far round the circle you can get before the children run out of ideas.

Equipment:
• Object related to topic

To make it easier:
• Children who are shy or have language problems may have difficulty thinking of something to say. In this situation, it is helpful to use 'phone-a-friend' which means they can select another child in the group to help them out.

To make it harder:
• Instead of just passing the object round, YOU have control of where the it goes. Tell the children 'You MUST keep listening because I might come back to you.' Then hand the object to random members of the group, repeatedly going back to any children who tend to switch off.

Ground Rules:
• You can only talk when you are holding the object.

Inside Information:
• This is a really useful way of brainstorming while incorporating good listening.
• This is a really nice activity for reinforcing and practising topic vocabulary.
• Again you will need to minimise the stress on children who might have language difficulties. You can use 'phone-a-friend' as described above, but also try to place children who might find this task a challenge near the beginning of the circle.

Listening to all the words – Game 7

Interactive stories

How to play:
For this activity you will need a big story book and matching pictures of the characters in the story. Give all the children one of the characters to hold. Say to the children 'I am going to read you a story but I am NOT going to show you the pictures. You have got to listen and when you hear your picture you have got to stand up and sit down again.'

Equipment:
• A big book and enough matching pictures of the characters for all class members

TIP: Story sacks might be suitable for use with smaller groups but you must make sure that all group members have an object to hold.

To make it easier:
• With Early Years children use simple stories with real objects.

To make it harder:
• Choose a story with a large cast of characters. This may mean that individual children will have to wait and keep listening for a long time before their character is mentioned.

Ground Rules:
• You cannot fiddle with your picture. You must keep it still.
• You can only stand up when you hear your picture.

Inside Information:
• This is a good game for children who tend to switch off or to copy others but you will need a story with a set of characters which are repeated at intervals so that children cannot switch off.
• It is fine to give more than one child a picture of the same character but you must mix them up so that children cannot copy the child sitting next to them.
• Make sure you take time to go through all the characters before you read the story, so that everyone knows who they are.
• Good stories to use are:

  ➤ Each Peach Pear Plum
  ➤ Billy's Beetle
  ➤ The Gingerbread Man
  ➤ The Giant Turnip

Listening to all the words – Game 8

Is it me?

How to play:
The idea of this game is that children must listen to two statements and decide whether they apply to themselves before carrying out an action. This is a good game to move children from one activity to another in a calm and orderly fashion. E.g. 'If you are a boy and you are 8 … line up at the door.' However, you can also play the game with dressing up props. E.g. 'If you are a girl and you are wearing black shoes … put on a hat.'

Equipment:
• None necessary, but to make it fun you could use a set of dressing up props – suitable for boys and girls, e.g. hats, hairbands, glasses, medals, necklaces, sweatbands, etc.

To make it easier:
• Use very concrete statements, e.g. gender/age/clothing.
• Don't use props and only have one action – e.g. 'If you are boy and you are 6 … line up at the door.'

To make it harder:
• Use more abstract statements, e.g. hair/eye colour; likes/dislikes.
• Give the children 3 statements to listen to. E.g. 'If you are a boy AND you are wearing trainers AND you have a sister … put on some glasses.'

Ground Rules:
• You must not move until you have listened to ALL of the words.

Inside Information:
• This is a really good game for those children who listen to the first thing you say and then think they know what to do. If they start to move once they have heard the first statement then remind them to stop and listen right to the end before they decide whether or not it is them.
• Always start with concrete statements where there can be no arguments. Eye colour can provoke a huge amount of debate, which stops children doing good listening.
• You can introduce concepts that you may be working on in other areas of the curriculum. E.g. 'If you are MORE than 6 and you have trousers on.'

Listening to all the words – Game 9

The silly shaker

How to play:
Start by explaining to the children what a nonsense word is. E.g. 'A nonsense word is a silly word which doesn't mean anything – like stiggleflump.' Give the first child in the circle a shaker and explain that you are going to read a little story with lots of nonsense words in it. Every time they hear a silly word they must shake the silly shaker and pass it on to the next child.

Equipment:
• Nonsense sentences, paragraphs or stories (appendix 13)
• Shaker

To make it easier:
• Just give each child one sentence each with one nonsense word. They have to shake the silly shaker when they hear it.

To make it harder:
• Read a nonsense story. The children have to shake when they hear the nonsense word and pass it on to the next child. Keep passing the shaker around the group until the story is finished.
• See if the child can think of a real word that would go in the sentence instead of the nonsense word.

Ground Rules:
• Only shake the shaker when you hear the nonsense word.

Inside Information:
• Many children with receptive language difficulties become used to not understanding and never ask for an explanation. This is a really good game for getting children to realise that there are some words that they know and some words that they don't know.
• If you want to encourage children to ask for clarification, follow up this game by telling the children that sometimes grown-ups might use words they don't know and ask what they should do if that happens. This gives you the opportunity to model saying 'What does that word mean?' Give children lots of praise for using this strategy in class.

Listening to all the words – Game 10

Do as I say not as I do

How to play:
This is a variation on 'Simon Says' or 'Follow the leader'. In this version of the game you have to say one action but carry out a different one. The children must do as you say, not do as you do. Children who copy your action instead of listening to the instruction are out. The winner is the last person still in the game.

Equipment:
· None needed but a prompt sheet is included in appendix 15.

To make it easier:
· Just give the children one instruction at a time.

To make it harder:
· Link together a sequence of instructions without pausing.

Ground Rules:
· You must do what the leader says and not copy the action they are doing.
· When you are out you must sit quietly and put your hand up if you see anyone getting it wrong.

Inside Information:
· Do not underestimate how difficult this game is to lead. Unless you are very confident that you can say one action and do another, use the prompt sheet.
· You may also need another adult to help spot children who were caught out.

9 Adapting the environment so that children can listen

There are many factors in the school environment that can affect all children's ability to keep listening. As adults, we are all generally more capable of keeping focused (and not getting distracted) than the children we work with. Children's listening can be affected by many things that we successfully screen out as adults and therefore it is not always easy to recognise what is distracting children in school. In our work in schools we have found that changes in the following areas can make real improvements in children's listening.

Noise levels in school

Background noise can have a significant impact on any child's ability to listen in school. We can, however, exert influence over the major source of noise in a classroom – the children themselves – in order to ensure it is at an appropriate level. Research undertaken by Shield and Dockerell (2004) in London primary schools has shown that, when listening to speech, all children are more affected by background noise than adults. Children with special educational needs are even more affected than typically developing children. Maintaining background noise at an appropriate level in class will improve the chances of all children to keep listening.

In order for children to be able to screen out background noise effectively, adults need to be speaking at a level 15 to 20 decibels above the background noise. The World Health Organization recommends that noise levels in class should be no more than 35 decibels. If noise levels rose to around 55 decibels, adults would need to speak at 75 decibels to enable all children to screen out the background noise effectively. This level is the equivalent of busy traffic noise or a vacuum cleaner. Teaching staff who regularly speak at this volume are likely to develop persistent voice problems because of the strain this can put on their vocal cords. (As speech and language therapists, we know that teachers are the biggest client group for our colleagues who specialise in voice problems.) Shield and Dockerell's research found that the average noise levels generated by children and activities in the schools they visited were up to 75 decibels. These findings were mirrored in research done by the Canadian Association of Speech-Language Pathologists and Audiologists in Scottish schools, which found that more than 90 per cent of the normal classrooms had inadequate listening conditions.

This study of 1162 students, aged 5 to 9 years old found lessons typically took place in a noise of around 60 decibels, which was produced by the chattering of the children and the humming sound from fluorescent lights, heating, air conditioning systems, fish tanks and computers. In these conditions, children were missing as many as one word in six (Greenfield 2007).

Establishing appropriate levels of noise

Children who are poor listeners need help to recognise what is an appropriate level of noise for working and listening in class. To help them learn, we need to draw their attention to when noise levels are appropriate, rather than telling them when it is too noisy. When doing this, it can also be helpful to remind children that, because they are quiet, this is helping everyone to do good listening. A simple way for adults to recognise an appropriate noise level is to see if they can talk to the children they are working with without raising their voice.

Using a sound toy (like a bell or tambourine) or a visual prompt (such as waving hands in the air – a prompt that children join in, and learn that this means 'be quiet') can be an effective way of establishing quiet. These can also help to prevent adults putting their voices under strain by having to raise their voices to do this.

Seating

It is easier for children to keep listening when sitting on chairs.

After working with thousands of children of all ages, we can both say this with confidence. This is supported by evidence from our occupational therapy colleagues.

However, in school children are often asked to sit on the floor and keep listening during a lesson. This makes the whole process of listening much more challenging. Many children in school have not developed sufficient trunk control to sit on the floor. They need something to lean against so that they can concentrate on listening rather than needing to focus on staying upright and sitting still. Giving them the support of an appropriately sized chair (where their feet can be flat on the floor and hips and knees are at 90-degree angles) frees up their attention and allows them to listen much more effectively.

All teachers have had the experience of asking a class to come and sit on the carpet and then finding children who try and squeeze into a non-existent space in a row, or sit on top of another child. Our occupational therapist colleagues tell us that many primary aged children do not have the spatial/depth perception to organise finding (and staying in) a space on the floor. These children invade the personal space of others and, as well as struggling to keep listening themselves, distract other children. Putting children on chairs helps to organise each child's personal space, and reduces distractions for the whole class.

When it is not possible for all children to be sitting on chairs in class when they need to listen, the following suggestions may help.

- Putting a carpet tile down in the listening space for each child to sit on allows everyone to have an appropriate space to sit and listen. Named carpet tiles (that the teacher organises in an appropriate format) also help to prevent arguments about who wants to sit next to each other. This can help focus the whole class more quickly.
- When this is not possible, have a row of 'good listening' carpet tiles at the front of the listening area for the children who find it hardest to organise their own sitting. This can also prevent them from distracting other children. Alternatively, have a row of chairs at the back of the listening area for the poorest listeners to improve their chances of sitting still and staying focused.
- When children are regularly being asked to sit on the floor, using photographs can help. Try assembling the class in your ideal group mix, putting the children you need at the front, separating children who

distract each other and ensuring everyone is sitting in a space. Then take a photograph of the class doing their best sitting and looking. Blow the photograph up and display it next to your sitting area. This is the seating plan that children have to follow every time they come and sit on the carpet. You can change these every few weeks if appropriate. The photograph helps children to organise where and how to sit, and can also prevent arguments about who wants to sit next to each other.

Research on how children sit in class

Hastings and Chantry-Wood (2000) summarised 20 years of research on seating arrangements for children in class and found that the listening of children could significantly improve when changes were made. They reached the following conclusions from reviewing the research.

- Almost all children's attention to their individual work increases when they sit in pairs, or seating arrangements where no-one sits opposite them.
- Sitting in rows or a horseshoe arrangements where every child can face the speaker improves the listening of the whole class
- The children who made the biggest progress in listening when seating arrangements were changed were the ones who were previously most easily distracted.

When we share these findings with teachers we often get the response that in class children are seated in groups around tables (rather than in rows) in order to facilitate interaction and co-operation between children during group work. However, research findings from the same review showed that, in studies of teacher/pupil interactions, group work accounted for only 10–20% of all learning during the school day. At other times, children were sitting in groups but carrying out individual tasks. It may be more helpful to have a seating arrangement in class that improves everyone's listening for the majority of the timetable, and move chairs and tables into a group formation only for those times when children are carrying out group tasks together.

How learning breaks can help

As adults we have all experienced the challenge of trying to listen during a training course. It becomes harder to keep listening the longer the session goes on. Once we have had a break it is always easier to focus on the speaker. It is also easier to keep listening if we know that a planned break is timetabled into the session and is going to happen soon. Applying the same principles to children's listening in class can result in real improvements. A learning break only needs to last two minutes. Afterwards children are always more able to keep listening. Incorporating a brief learning break into a lesson (and letting children know when this will happen) allows them to pace their listening and means they are more likely to keep focused. Figures 9.1 and 9.2 show what can happen to children's concentration during the course of a lesson and the impact a learning break can have on their ability to keep listening.

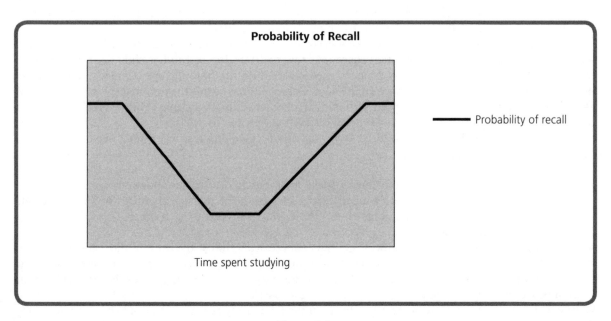

Figure 9.1

Figure 9.1 shows that learners are more likely to recall the first and last information that they heard and least likely to remember the information in the middle of the lesson. Unfortunately, this is usually where the key information is contained.

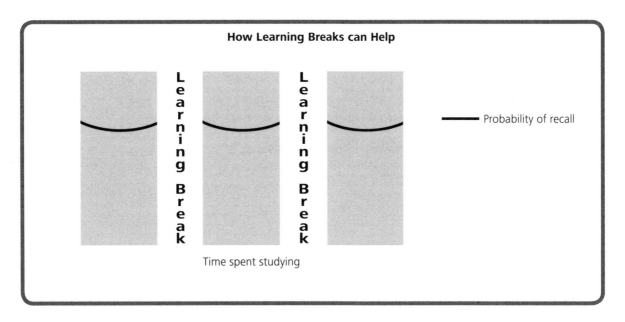

Figure 9.2

Figure 9.2 shows how learning breaks can combat this by reducing the extent of the mid-lesson 'dip' in listening and recall.

The most important thing about any kind of learning break is that it should involve getting up and moving about. For younger children try doing an action song during a break. For older children brain gym activities, running on the spot or other physical exercise for two minutes, will mean they are more able to concentrate when the lesson starts again. Getting a drink or helping to move chairs (if the format of the lesson involves moving from listening as a whole class to working in groups) could also be appropriate activities.

Photographs

Using photographs in class helps children remember the rules and modify their own behaviour to carry them out.

- Take photographs of the class carrying out each of the four rules and display these alongside the listening prompt cards. It is very important to take photographs of good listening in more than one context. E.g. sitting still on the carpet, in their groups, in assembly, etc. as this helps children to generalise the skills that they have learnt and recognise that good listening is important throughout school.
- For individual children supported by teaching assistants where listening is a target, use a photo fan with the four rules, illustrated by photos of the child carrying them out. The TA can then show a photograph to remind the child of the target behaviour non-verbally during whole-class activities. This is much less disruptive than having verbally to refocus a child's attention while a teacher is talking. The fan can also travel with the child to different environments in school as a reminder. It is important that the fan remains a tool for the teaching assistant rather than being given to the child who may find it a distraction.

Withdrawal from class

In school, we often take children who need small group work (and who find listening particularly difficult) out of the classroom into environments where there are more distractions and fewer opportunities to control them. There may be a case for organising the class so that the most able listeners are the ones who work in the most challenging environment. However, if this is not possible, it is helpful to carry out a listening 'audit' of the environment with the children. This will help them to take on a greater responsibility for their own listening. For example:

- What things could stop us doing good looking and listening?
  (people walking along the corridor, doors opening, music from the hall)

- Where could we sit/put our chairs to help us do good listening?
  (with our back to the corridor, door; next to the teacher; etc.)

- What are we going to do if the door opens?
  (keep looking at the teacher)

10 How to talk so children will listen

The kind of language which adults use when talking to children can make a real difference to how well children listen. Children can easily switch off for a number of reasons:

- too much information for children to process in one go
- ambiguous language which can confuse the message the adult is trying to convey
- specific concepts which are difficult to understand
- trigger phrases which stop the child listening to anything else in an instruction.

Keeping it simple

1. Reducing the load

Children are more likely to keep listening if instructions are short and easy to understand. Compare:

In a moment the bell will be going for breaktime so, before you get your fruit, I want you to finish the sentence you are writing and then line up at the door.

with:

Finish your sentence.
Line up at the door.

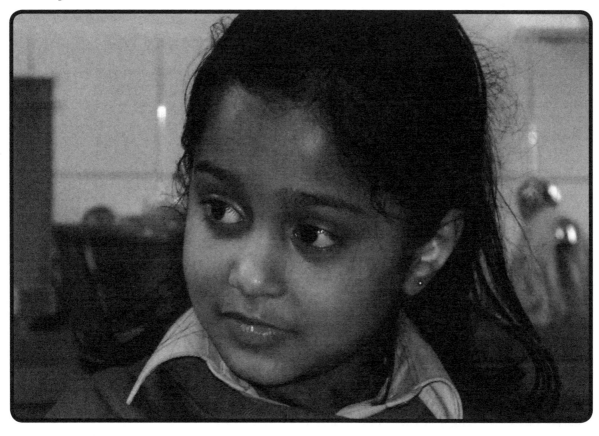

We often use an introductory sentence when giving an instruction which doesn't contain any useful information.

It's nearly time to stop writing, so I would like you to make sure you have put the date on your work.

The important information in this instruction is in the final six words but the speaker has used so many words first that many children will have stopped listening before they get to this point.

2. Telling, not asking

As adults we often sound as if we are asking children a question when we are really giving them an instruction. Consider the following examples:

Would you like to come and sit on the carpet?

Can you come and do your reading book with me?

Please can you log off the computer now?

There are two difficulties with this. Firstly, it increases the number of words that children have to listen to. Secondly, it implies that there is a choice of response – children can choose whether to sit on the carpet or not – when this is obviously not the case.

3. Keeping it concrete

English is a language which is rich in idiom and figures of speech but these can make it hard for children to listen. Children on the autistic spectrum particularly find non-literal language difficult, but many other children will also be confused by this type of language. For example,

It's driving me up the wall. – Something to do with a car accident?

He's feeling under the weather. – Did he get wet in the rain?

II'm running late. – Are they doing PE?

4. Minding your manners

We all want to model good manners when we are speaking to children but this often makes us use extra language by phrasing instructions as questions. 'Please' also has an implicit meaning that the request is optional. To avoid these difficulties while still being polite, it is better to give the instruction and add 'thank you'. 'Thank you' implies that the instruction will be carried out.
Compare these two instructions:

Please could you come and sit on the carpet?

Sit on the carpet. Thank you.

5. Avoiding before and after

'Before' and 'after' are two of the most confusing terms in English because they change the order of an instruction without changing the order of the words. Even normally developing children do not acquire these concepts until about six years of age but many other children do not understand them until much later. Consider this example:

Before you go have your snack, you need to finish your writing.

As adults we understand that the word 'before' means that the child needs to finish the writing first and then have a snack. However, a child who does not understand 'before' will just follow the sentence order and think that snack time is coming first. The same difficulty arises with 'after':

We are going out to play after we have finished maths.

A child who does not understand 'after' will think that playtime is coming next, followed by maths and will be confused (and disappointed!) when this does not happen. It is possible to use 'before' and 'after' with the right sentence order, e.g. *After we have finished our maths, we will go out to play.* However, this requires so much thought that, when giving more than one instruction, it is probably better to avoid 'before' and 'after' and use 'first' and 'next'. E.g. *First finish maths, next playtime.*

6. Watching out for trigger phrases

There are some phrases, which when they are included, mean that children listen to nothing else in that instruction. Examples of trigger phrases are:

Line up at the door.

It's nearly playtime.

Time for assembly.

Everyone who works with children will know what the trigger phrases are for their particular group. The key to managing trigger phrases is never to use them in conjunction with any other information. Only say them when there is nothing else you want the children to do.

7. Giving whole class instructions

When teachers give instructions like 'Can everyone get their reading book' there are some children who do not respond. They do not have the concept of everyone meaning them too. When this happens, these children need to be named specifically alongside 'everyone' to ensure they listen and carry out the task, e.g. 'Can everyone and Matthew get their reading book.' This may sound odd but eventually these children will learn what 'everyone' means and respond appropriately. You may need to use this strategy for some time before this happens.

8. Using unpredictability to keep children listening

In school we try to be scrupulously fair in ensuring everyone has a turn in an activity or answering a question. We often work our way methodically round a group of children to make sure this happens. This can, however, cause poor listening for two reasons. Children can switch off once they have had a turn as they know they won't get asked again. They can also not bother to listen while other children are talking as they can see they are going to get a turn eventually. Exploiting unpredictability can improve children's motivation to keep listening but you will need to be explicit about what you are going to do at the beginning of an activity. For example:

- 'I am going to point to you when I want you to answer a question so you need to watch me to see if you are next.' You will then need to point to children in a random order. This will encourage children to keep looking and listening as they have no other way of finding out if it is their turn next.
- 'Even if you have a turn I might choose you again so you need to keep listening.' This encourages children to keep listening throughout an activity but you must make sure you do choose someone again so they can see why it is important not to switch off.
- 'We are going to use the **same** apparatus today but we are going to do a **different** maths task. You will need to listen carefully so you know what to do.' Using the same equipment for a different task (and being explicit about this at the beginning of an activity) encourages those children who normally switch off (as they think they know what to do already and don't need to listen!) to keep listening.

Looking at instructions

On the following pages are some examples of instructions that might be used with children. We have highlighted the potential difficulties and suggested alternative ways of giving the instruction. Reflecting on how we give instructions can be a useful training activity and some of these instructions are reproduced in appendix 14, so that they can be used for staff discussion.

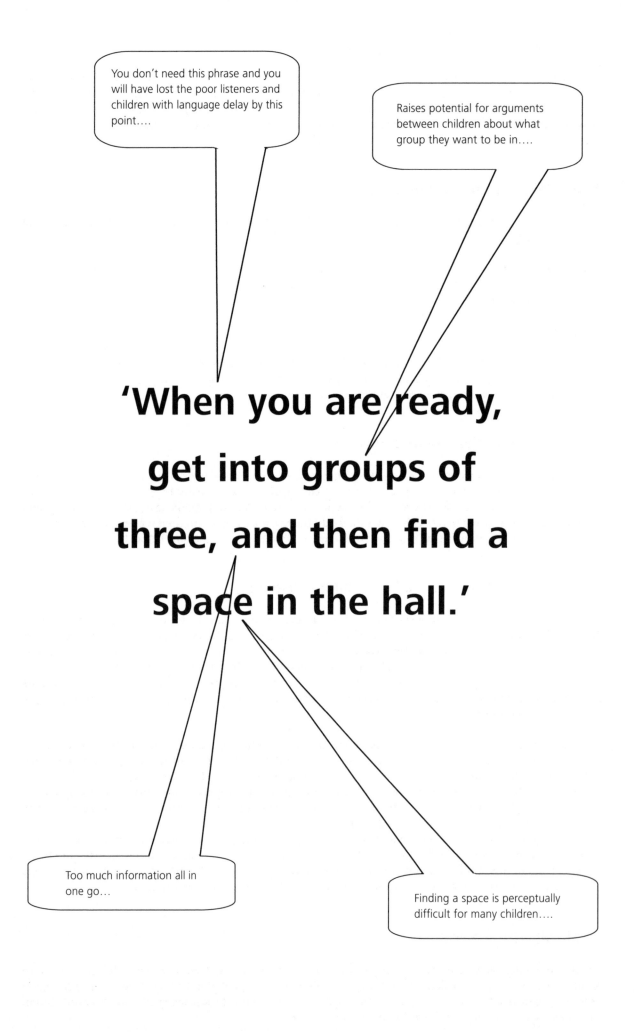

You don't need this phrase and you will have lost the poor listeners and children with language delay by this point....

Raises potential for arguments between children about what group they want to be in....

'When you are ready, get into groups of three, and then find a space in the hall.'

Too much information all in one go...

Finding a space is perceptually difficult for many children....

Suggested alternative:

> Get into groups
> of three ...

And get a group of three children together to SHOW what you mean.

You are actually enquiring about the child's ability to turn around so you may get children who say 'yes' but don't turn around.

Not explicit enough. You may get children who turn all the way round and are still facing the wrong way!

'Can you turn around please?'

Many children won't understand the implied meaning which is that you want them to look at you.

Suggested alternatives:

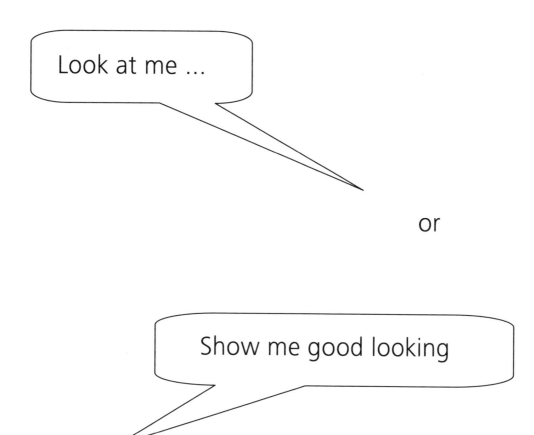

Look at me ...

or

Show me good looking

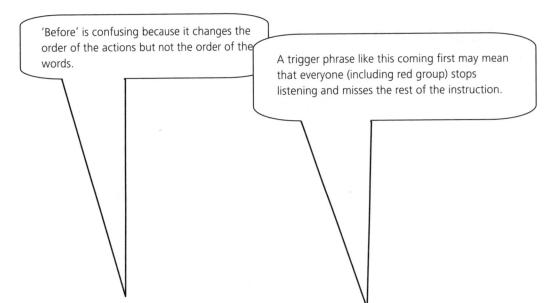

'Before' is confusing because it changes the order of the actions but not the order of the words.

A trigger phrase like this coming first may mean that everyone (including red group) stops listening and misses the rest of the instruction.

'Before we move back to our tables can red group fetch their reading books?'

When you embed information which only applies to one group, within an instruction, you run the risk that everyone will do it, not just red group.

Suggested alternative:

Red group – get your
reading books …

… Pause …

Everyone – back to
your tables now.

This is redundant language – the children can't write the answer if they don't know it!

'If you know the answer, write it on your whiteboard but don't let anyone else see it.'

Negatives are a real challenge for children with hearing or language difficulties. Say what you DO want them to do instead.

This is redundant language – if they have been given whiteboards then where else will they write it?

Suggested alternative:

> Write the answer.
> Hide it.

And model it yourself so that the children can see what to do.

This is ambiguous language which some children won't understand or will take literally.

This statement is not needed and will panic the panicky children who then won't listen to anything else.

'We are running out of time, so finish the question you are on then put your worksheets in a pile on your table.'

This is too much information all in one go. It needs to be broken into chunks.

Suggested alternative:

Finish the question you are on …

… Pause …

Put the worksheets in a pile on your table.

Trigger phrase.

'In a minute, the bell will go for assembly so finish your sentence and then line up at the door.'

A trigger phrase in an instruction means that many children will not pay attention to anything else.

Suggested alternative:

> Finish the question you are on…

… Pause …

> Line up for assembly.

The element of choice will overload many children's processing and stop them listening to anything else. This needs to be a separate instruction.

'Choose your favourite colour then draw me a circle that fills the whole of your page.'

This is a challenging perceptual concept. The only way to be sure that children know what to do is to have one you did earlier to show them.

Suggested alternative:

Choose your favourite colour ...

!

... Pause ...

Draw a circle that fills the whole page like this.

And have one you did earlier to show them.

This is a rhetorical question and many children will be confused by the implied meaning and not understand that they should NOT shout out. They may also feel that the question needs answering and shout 'yes' or 'no'.

'Do I want you to shout out the answer?'

Children who find lots of language hard to process will just respond to the last four words and shout out the answer.

Suggested alternative:

Put your hand up.

And finally …

We can all recognise when children are poor at listening and the impact it can have on all their learning in school. When there are so many competing demands on our teaching time with children it can be hard to find time to work on improving listening. However, our experience has taught us that with direct and targeted input, it is possible to turn around children's listening skills in a relatively short space of time. A small amount of input can have a massive impact on their ability to listen and learn in school.

Class case history: Year 1 School S

Year 1 was a class of 25 children with the majority having English as an additional language. One child had a statement of special educational needs because of learning and behaviour difficulties. Two other children in class also had challenging behaviour. These three children often disrupted lessons and, while their behaviour was being addressed, other children in the class found it difficult to keep listening and stay focused on tasks.

Direct work on listening helped this class in two ways. Firstly, the statemented child made real progress in understanding what good listening meant, and in modifying his own behaviour in class to carry out the rules of good listening. He became more motivated to participate in class activities and the disruptive episodes of behaviour became much less frequent. The two other boys with challenging behaviour also showed improved listening and, following direct listening work, all three were rated as having only moderate listening difficulties. Secondly, the whole class became much more able to keep listening during episodes of disruptive behaviour. Their teacher explained, 'Previously interruptions through behaviour issues affected everyone's listening and progress in class. Following direct listening work I was able to say to the class "Can everyone keep doing good listening" when a child tried to disrupt the lesson. Children understood what this meant and their improved listening meant they could ignore interruptions and keep focused. This had a major impact on the progress of children in my class.' This teacher was so impressed at the effect of the project on her class that she persuaded her head teacher to fund the same input into all five classes in school the following year.

Case history: Jack

Jack was six years old and in Year 2 when we worked with his class. He had been experiencing some difficulties settling into school and was showing signs of emotional and behavioural disturbance. At the start of the project, Jack was rated by his teacher as having severe listening difficulties, scoring only 4 on the listening rating scale. He was one of the younger children in the year and had very low self-confidence. This resulted in him disengaging from any activity which he felt was too challenging for him. At these times he would withdraw eye contact, turn away from the group and often disturb other children. This had a very significant effect on his ability to learn and he was under-performing both in literacy and numeracy. He received additional help both within class and in regular small groups. However, his poor listening prevented him from benefiting fully from this additional support.

At the beginning of the direct work, Jack was often unresponsive and frequently opted out. However, as the weeks progressed, his participation increased and his confidence grew. He was able to demonstrate some good listening skills. The praise he got for this good listening was not related to any academic success and had a profound effect on his self-esteem. He became more engaged and crucially was more willing to try new tasks even if they were challenging for him. At the end of the intervention his listening score had increased to 8.5. However, when we revisited the school a term later he had continued to improve and his teacher rated him with a listening score of 11. Not only had his listening improved but the success he was experiencing had helped him to be happier and more confident in school.

Case history: Ethan

Ethan was 8 years old and in Year 3 when we worked with his class. He has a statement of special educational needs and a diagnosis of autistic spectrum disorder. His teacher rated Ethan as having severe listening difficulties. He stayed quiet in class but scored the lowest rating on looking and listening to all of the words. During whole-class activities Ethan actively withdrew from listening and found it difficult to interact with other children during group work.

Following direct work on listening his teacher now rated Ethan as having adequate listening skills. His eye contact with both adults and children improved. Ethan was able to keep listening more consistently in whole-class activities and was much more able to follow whole-class instructions without needing individual attention from the teacher to check he had listened to information. Ethan was now more able to participate actively during group activities in class, and listen and respond to other children's contributions. He also started to recognise when he had not understood an instruction, and spontaneously ask for help or clarification from school staff.

Case history: Ryan

Ryan was 6 years old when we worked with his class. He has a statement of special educational needs because of his challenging behaviour, and because of learning difficulties. His teacher rated him as having severe listening difficulties, scoring the lowest rating on each of the four rules of listening. Before we worked with his class, Ryan was following a largely differentiated curriculum and was working one-to-one with his teaching assistant for much of the day as he found it very challenging to listen in whole-class activities and to participate in group work. His challenging behaviour affected the ability of other children in class to keep listening.

Direct work on listening enabled Ryan to understand what good listening behaviour was. By the end of the six weeks he wanted to participate, and could modify his own behaviour in order to be chosen for an activity. His teacher now rated Ryan as having only moderate listening difficulties in class. The impact of this on Ryan's learning and behaviour in class was significant. His teaching assistant was now able to support Ryan's learning within the classroom. Ryan could stay focused when sitting on the carpet during whole-class work, and his improving self-esteem meant he was happy to be chosen to come to the front of the class to take a turn in interactive learning tasks. It was no longer necessary to differentiate the style and content of most of the curriculum for Ryan as his improved behaviour meant he could access the activities in the lower ability group in class. Ryan's less disruptive behaviour also improved the listening environment for the rest of the children in class and enabled them to keep focused during activities.

Good listening is

Looking at the person who is talking.

Good listening is Sitting still.

Good listening is staying quiet.

Good listening is

Listening to ALL the words.

APPENDIX 2 – LISTENING SKILLS RATING SCALE

www.continuumbooks.com/resources/9781441174765

	Score	1	2	3	4
Sitting still		Not able to stay on chair/floor Constant fidgeting	Inappropriate sitting posture/ lots of fidgeting	Stays on chair/ floor but some fidgeting	Appropriate balanced sitting
Looking at the person who is talking		Does not initiate eye contact spontaneously	Some eye contact but not sustained	Initiates eye contact but needs recall	Appropriate eye contact when listening
Staying quiet		Consistently interrupts/talks during instructions	Occasionally quiet but cannot maintain this	Some talking but can be recalled to stay quiet and listen	Quiet when listening in class
Listening to all of the words		Does not follow instructions/ relies on routine/ copies others Does not recognise when has not understood	Carries out part of an instruction – needs repeated reminders	Follows simple instructions but needs repetition of complex information	Able to listen to complex/ unfamiliar information
			Recognises when has not listened accurately and seeks help		
Total listening score:					

LISTENING SKILLS RATING SCALE – CLASS

Name:	Sitting still:	Looking at the person talking:	Staying quiet:	Listening to all the words:	Listening score:
1					
2					
3					
4					
5					
6					
7					
8					
9					
10					
11					
12					
13					
14					
15					
16					
17					
18					
19					
20					
21					
22					
23					
24					
25					
26					
27					
28					
29					
30					
				TOTAL:	

APPENDIX 3 – CLASS LISTENING PROFILE

Total listening score for class:	
Divided by number in class:	
Average Listening Score for class:	

Number of pupils scoring:	Total ____ x 100 Class Size	Percentage of class with:
Below 8	____ x 100	Severe listening difficulties:
8–11	____ x 100	Moderate listening difficulties:
12 or above	____ x 100	Adequate listening:

APPENDIX 4 – OUR LISTENING WORK – INFORMATION FOR PARENTS

Listening is a special kind of attention – to listen we have to pay attention to sounds. Many children who have problems with listening are good with other kinds of attention. They may be able to sit and watch their favourite video for a long time or they may be able to concentrate for ages on their favourite toy. However, a child who has difficulties with listening may have problems with:

- listening to stories, especially in a group
- listening to you explaining something
- waiting for their turn in a conversation or a game.

Listening is a really important skill for learning language but it is also a very important skill at school. A good listener at school is more likely to take part in class discussions, remember what they have learned and understand what they have to do. In fact – if you're a good listener, you are more likely to be a good learner.

As you've probably discovered, just telling children to 'listen!' does not really help very much. This is because listening is quite a hard thing to do. It's not just one skill – it is several skills. In our work on listening, we aim to help the children learn the skills that make up good listening.

Our four rules of 'Good Listening' are:

- **Looking** at the person who's talking.
- **Keeping still**
- **Keeping quiet**
- **Listening** to all the words

You can also help by reminding your child about these rules during the everyday things you do together that need them to listen. You can try:

- **Reminding them of the rule before you need them to listen:**
  E.g. 'I've got a surprise for you. When you're quiet, I'll tell you what it is.'
  'Look at me – where are your shoes?'
  'I'm going to read a story. You need to keep really still so you can do good listening.'

- **Praising them when you can see them using the skills:**
  E.g. 'Well done, you kept really quiet and that helped you to do good listening.'
  'Great, I can see your eyes so I know you're ready to listen to me.'
  'Brilliant! You listened right to the end!'

- **Being specific about what they're doing wrong when they're not listening:**
  E.g. 'You're talking at the same time as me – that makes it very hard for you to do good listening.'

This will really help them to use their new skills in real life.

APPENDIX 5 – LISTENING GROUP PLAN

	Week 1	Week 2	Week 3	Week 4	Week 5	Week 6
Looking	Who looks different? (obvious changes)	Who looks different? (Subtle changes)	Who feels different? (happy/cross)	Who feels different? (happy/ cross/ surprised)	Who feels different? (happy/ cross/ surprised/ sad)	Pass the turn – child led e.g. T-Rocks
Listening	Who, what, where?	Fruit salad	Is it me?	Colours of the rainbow	Semantic categories	Interactive story
Staying quiet	Sound location with boxes	Sound location with radio hidden in room	Giant's keys	Sound location with ticking 'bomb'	Giant's treasure	Keys around the circle
Keeping Still	Sitting still with musical instruments & pecking bird and stop/go sign	Fidget monitor	Fidget monitor	Sitting still on mats with timer	Sitting still on mats with timer with bubbles as distractor	Sitting still on mats with timer with feather dusters as distractor
Additional:	Pass the turn game: e.g. Ali Baba's camel	Pass the turn game: e.g. Ker Plunk	Pass the turn game: e.g. No Fleas on Fred	Pass the turn game: e.g. Shark Bait	Pass the turn game: e.g. Pick up Sticks	Certificates

APPENDIX 6 – EMOTION PICTURES

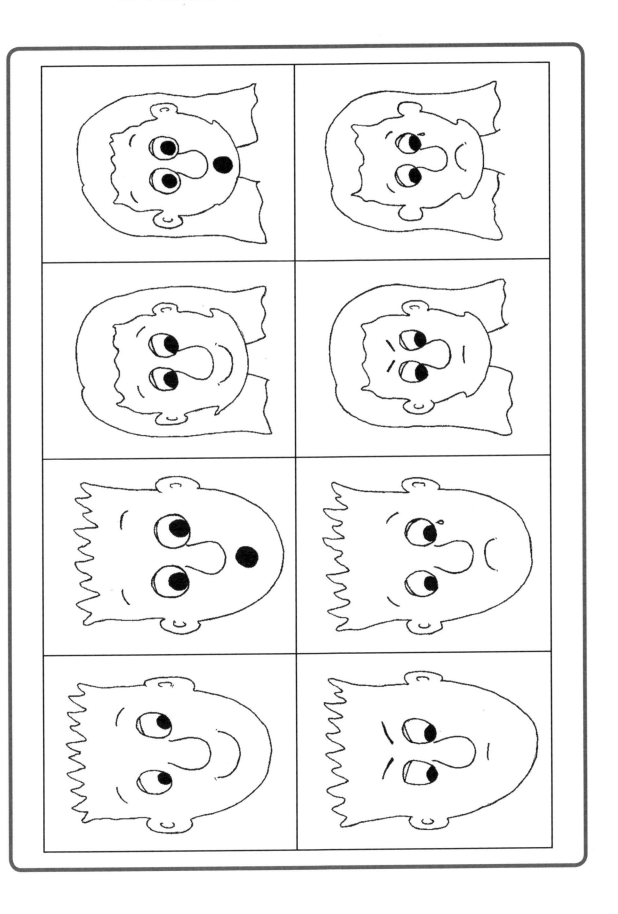

Cross Boy

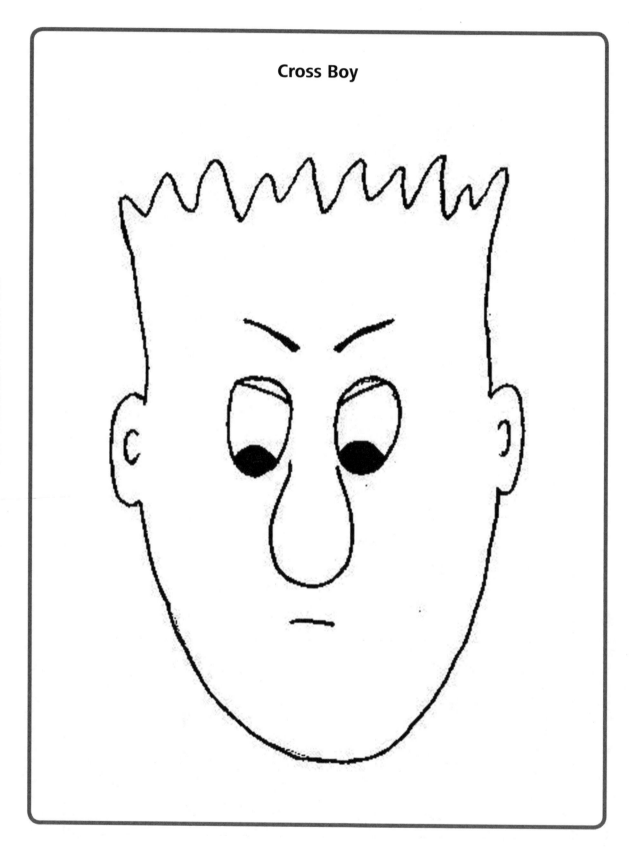

Happy Boy

Sad Boy

Surprised Boy

Cross Girl

Happy Girl

Sad Girl

Surprised Girl

APPENDIX 7 – BLINKING PICTURE

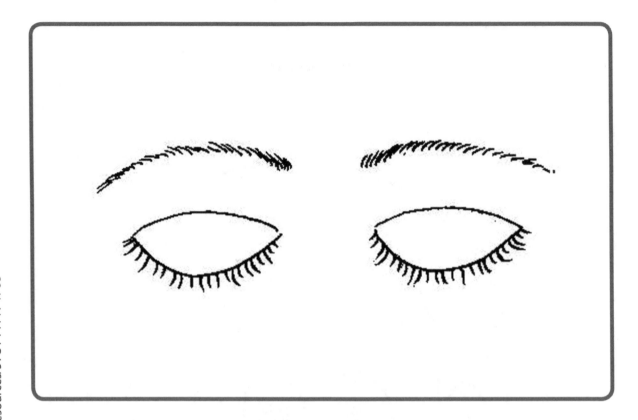

APPENDIX 8 – LEADER PICTURE

I'm the Leader

APPENDIX 9 – STOP/GO SIGNS
(COLOUR VERSIONS OF THESE IMAGES ARE AVAILABLE ONLINE FOR DOWNLOAD)

www.continuumbooks.com/resources/9781441174765

APPENDIX 10 – FIDGET MONITOR AND FIDGET

Fidget Monitor

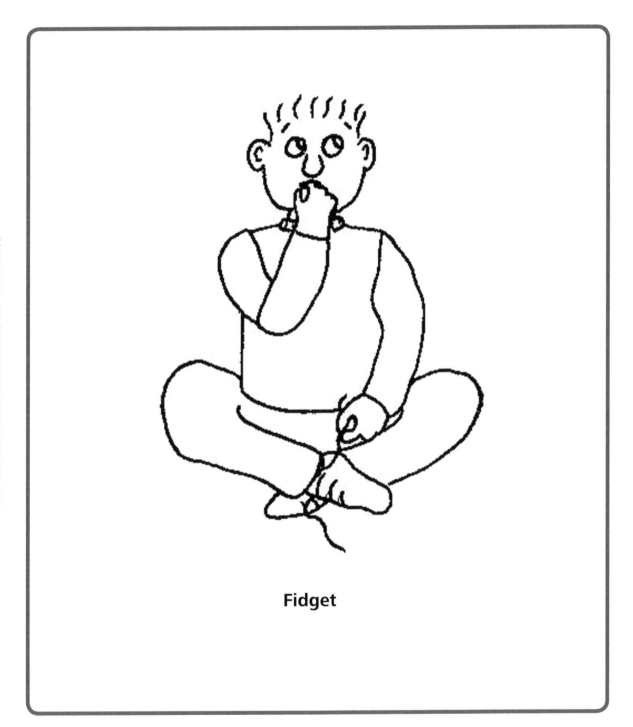

Fidget

APPENDIX 11 – SECRET MESSAGES

Secret messages

I'm hungry

?

Secret messages

I'm cross

?

Secret messages

I'm cold

?

Secret messages

Hello

?

Secret messages

I'm happy

?

Secret messages

I'm hot

?

Secret messages

I love you

?

Secret messages

I'm bored

?

Secret messages

I feel sick

?

Secret messages

It's raining

?

Secret messages

Where's my cup

?

Secret messages

It's time to go

?

Secret messages

I want the toilet

?

Secret messages

I don't understand

?

Secret messages

What time is it?

?

Secret messages

Shut the door

?

Secret messages

It's too noisy

?

Secret messages

Go away

?

Secret messages

My head hurts

?

Secret messages

That smells horrible

?

APPENDIX 12 – WHAT AM I?

What am I?

I am round…
You can play with me…
People throw me and kick me…

What am I?

I have a face…
I have two hands…
You need me to tell the time…

What am I?

I have 4 legs…
I have a tail…
You get milk from me…

What am I?

I have two arms…
I am made of wool…
You can wear me…

What am I?

I can hop…
I have a long powerful tail…
I carry my baby in a pouch…

What am I?

I am long and thin…
You hold me in your hand…
I have ink inside me…

What am I?

I am round…
You can eat me…
I am green and grow on trees…

What am I?

I am made of metal…
I have wheels and doors…
You can drive me…

What am I?

You find me in the garden…
I smell nice…
I have petals and leaves…

What am I?

You can see me in the sky…
I have wings…
I have an engine…

What am I?

I am made of paper…
I have a cover…
You can read me…

What am I?

I can help you to travel…
I have two wheels…
I have pedals…

What am I?

I can hop…
I have long ears…
I like to eat carrots…

What am I?

I am made of wool…
I am long and thin…
You wear me round your neck…

What am I?

I live on a farm…
I have a four legs and a tail…
I am pink…

What am I?

I am made of glass…
You can open me…
You can look out of me…

What am I?

I have numbers on me…
I make a ringing noise…
You can speak to your friends on me…

What am I?

I can fly…
I am an insect…
I make honey…

What am I?

You find me in the kitchen…
I have an electrical plug…
You put water in me…

What am I?

I am made of metal…
I help you to eat your dinner…
I am very sharp…

What am I?	What am I?
I am a ball	I am a clock

What am I?	What am I?
I am a cow	I am a jumper

What am I?	What am I?
I am a kangaroo	I am a pen

What am I?	What am I?
I am an apple	I am a car

What am I?	What am I?
I am a flower	I am a plane

What am I?

I am a book

What am I?

I am a bike

What am I?

I am a rabbit

What am I?

I am a scarf

What am I?

I am a pig

What am I?

I am a window

What am I?

I am a phone

What am I?

I am a bee

What am I?

I am a kettle

What am I?

I am a knife

www.continuumbooks.com/resources/9781441174765

APPENDIX 13 –
NONSENSE SENTENCES AND PARAGRAPHS

Sentences:

1. The little bear sat in the loodlemoud.

2. What are you going to spiggledock in the cake?

3. In the morning they shaveydibbed down the hill to the shops.

4. The jibblymave man laughed at the clowns.

5. In the woods the girls looked for a treezlepib to take home.

6. She lost the key, so she twikledeepoked on the door.

7. The teacher said 'It's too popply in this classroom.'

8. The clekelty car bumped into the wall and stopped.

9. All of the flajels came out from behind the clouds.

10. The man looked down the dark hole and saw a great big dobado.

Paragraphs:

In the morning, Ben looked at the spidkeedle. He was surprised to see its needosooks looked dirty. 'What have you been traggerling?' he said. The bear did not answer, so Tonerboz picked him up and put him in the hiddypiddy. Round and grenditch went the bear until he felt groggerly all over his dobax. 'I wish this would aveldoot', he said and just then he heard a veetimp.

When cooking bildeyhoffs, first you need to sieve some volpeyhind and add a pinch of gracklenubb. Crack a robble-tobble in a bowl and lecklemunch with a fork. Add to the tindeymipe, stirring all the fampo. Next measure a droogle of milk and trissleyclunk into the mixture. Leave to premp for about thirty clintoes.

A long time ago, denkoes did not have stoobles so they went everywhere on tabblings. The streets were rempled but it took too much jawbydosh to get to pralinkot. If it rained, the children would put on their craxozob and deshel-peshel through the puddles. At night, everyone would flishlinkle and nardogunt until it was dark.

Nonsense Word Story

Once upon a time, there was a little fleezlepog called Red Nibdib Hood. One day, her dobnicko was poorly. So her mother said 'Dindlehag, take these flowers and drenkeypitch to Grandma but be careful. Go straight to shubberhond cottage and don't spoggleyhoot to any strangers along the tillabobs.'

However, the big pagglegrind wolf was listening outside and quickly ran to Grandma's cottage, went uzpotchy and gobbled her up. Her dressed in Grandma's jarberlunks, got into her trinkle and settled down to wait.

Red Riding Hood walked jebblydove along the path, through the jonkeyhaze and finally reached Grandma's cottage. She chackled at the door and went in. 'Oh podnib!' she said, when she sloevumped Grandma. 'Pankeydowd big ears you've got!' 'All the neckle to hear you with,' said Grandma. 'And what sneggerdrab eyes you've got!' 'Stopplenoop the better to see you with my dear.' 'And Grandma, what big kleeblegrids you've got!' 'All the better to pretterpink you with!' And with that the wolf cluverdissed out of bed with a growl.

But at that moment a woodcutter came oodrishing in and grabbed the wolf by the snally, swung him round and cut his copplebomb open. Out came Grandma. She haggle-baggled Red Riding Hood and the wolf went cripuntly into the woods.

'Thank you Mr Woodcutter,' said Grandma and Red Riding Hompeyfone and they all sat down for a cup of slendypank and some of Mum's spalooshy chocolate cake.

'When you are ready, get into groups of three, and then find a space in the hall.'

What are the potential problems?

How could you make it easier?

'If you know the answer, write it on your whiteboard but don't let anyone else see it.'

What are the potential problems?

How could you make it easier?

'We are running out of time, so finish the question you are on, then put your worksheets in a pile on your table.'

What are the potential problems?

How could you make it easier?

'In a minute, the bell will go for assembly so finish your sentence and then line up at the door.'

What are the potential problems?

How could you make it easier?

Instruction:	Action:
'Clap your hands'	Stamp your feet
Instruction:	Action:
'Pat your head'	Wave your hands
Instruction:	Action:
'Blink your eyes'	Tap your nose
Instruction:	Action:
'Tap your nose'	Blink your eyes
Instruction:	Action:
'Wave your hands'	Pat your head
Instruction:	Action:
'Stamp your feet'	Clap your hands

REFERENCES

Basic Skills Agency (2003) *Young Children's Skills on Entry to Education*, report is available free (in English and Welsh) from Basic Skills Agency publications on 0870 600 2400.

Bercow, J. (2008) *Review of Services for Children and Young People (0–19) with Speech, Language and Communication Need*, <http://www.dcsf.gov.uk/slcnaction/downloads/7771-DCSF-BERCOW.PDF>.

BMRB International (British Market Research Bureaux) (2004) *Increasing Screen Time is Leading to Inactivity of 11–15s*, Youth TGI Study.

Christakis, D.A., Zimmerman, F.J., DiGiuseppe, D.L. and McCarty, C.A. (2004) *Early Television Exposure and Subsequent Attentional Problems in Children, Journal of Paediatrics*, 113(4) 708–13.

Evans, Schmidt, M., Pempek, T.A., Kirkorian, H.L., Frankenfield Lund, A. and Anderson, D.R. (2008) *The Effects of Background Television on the Toy Play Behavior of Very Young Children, Child Development*, 79(4), 1137–51.

The Framework for Teaching Literacy (2006) <http://www.standards.dfes.gov.uk/primary/literacy>.

Greenfield, N. (2007) *Testing 1, 2, 3. Can You Hear Me? Times Educational Supplement Scotland*, 19 October.

Hastings, N. and Chantry-Wood, K. (2000) *Spacing for Learning in Primary Classrooms: Bridging the Gaps*, paper presented at the British Educational Research Association Conference.

Hollich, G., Newman, R.S. and Jusczyk, P.W. (2005) *Infants' Use of Synchronized Visual Information to Separate Streams of Speech, Child Development*, 76(3), 598–613.

I CAN (2006) *The Cost to the Nation of Children's Poor Communication*, I CAN Talk series, issue 2, <http://www.ican.org.uk>.

Kirkorian, H.L., Pempek, T.A., Murphy, L.A., Evans Schmidt, M. and Anderson, D.R. (in press) *The Impact of Background Television on Parent–Child Interaction, Child Development*.

Maxwell, L.E. and Evans, G.W. (2004) *Impact of Classroom Noise on Reading*, paper presented at 147th Acoustical Society of America meeting.

Murkoff, H., Eisenberg, A. and Hathaway, S. (2004) *What to Expect, the First Year* (2nd edition), London: Simon and Schuster.

Rideout, V., Roberts, D.F. and Foehr, U.G. (2005) *Generation M: Media in the Lives of 8–18 Year Olds*, Menlo Park, CA: Kaiser Family Foundation.

Rose, J. (2006) *Independent Review into the Teaching of Early Reading*, <http://www.standards.dfes.gov.uk/rosereview/report.pdf>.

Shield, B. and Dockerell, J. (2004) *External and Internal Noise Surveys of London Primary Schools, Journal of the Acoustical Society of America*, 115, 730.

LIST OF GAMES

SUBJECT INDEX